July 1957
Toni Intravaia
From Ann Choate
(Gudenstein)

Barter

Life has loveliness to sell,
   All beautiful and splendid things,
Blue waves whitened on a cliff,
   Soaring fire that sways and sings,
And children's faces looking up
Holding wonder like a cup.

Life has loveliness to sell,
   Music like a curve of gold,
Scent of pine trees in the rain,
   Eyes that love you, arms that hold,
And for your spirit's still delight,
Holy thoughts that star the night.

Spend all you have for loveliness,
   Buy it and never count the cost;
For one white singing hour of peace
   Count many a year of strife well lost,
And for a breath of ecstasy
Give all you have been, or could be.

Sara Teasdale

The Dance in Art

A Book of

DANCES, POEMS, PAINTINGS, SCULPTURE

and MUSIC

By

LUCY LAMPKIN, A.B.

Founder and Principal

of the

LUCY LAMPKIN SCHOOL OF THE DANCE AND RELATED ARTS

Athens, Georgia

J. FISCHER & BRO.

119 West 40th Street   New York, N. Y.

1935

Printed in United States of America

EILERT PRINTING COMPANY, INC.
318-326 W. 39TH ST., NEW YORK

Dedicated to

MY MOTHER AND FATHER

Whose Faith and Devotion
have ever been
A Light on my Path

Preface

THE DANCE IN ART was planned as a book of correlated material for teachers and students of the dance and related arts. The dance can be enriched by drawing upon other arts related to it. It can also be a fine medium of art education. I hope that this book will prove a source of inspiration to all teachers, students and lovers of art, and that they will derive from it, a small share of the joy that was mine in the writing and my students' in the dancing.

The sculptures chosen have crystallized a set of dance movements that could enrich any dancer's repertoire. These movements have been incorporated in several of the dances, among them, "Playing Statue", "Play", "The Three Graces" and "At the Museum". I have sought inspiration for the dance in many paintings. The dance, "Gossip" is largely pantomime, while "A Dance of Banners" is highly dramatic. In "Joy" the movements are danced to the accompaniment of the spoken lines of the poem. Several of the dances were inspired by poems, the poem creating the idea and mood for that particular dance. The Lullaby is danced to the accompaniment of the song, while the March represents the mechanical stylized movement of the Modern School. The music chosen is largely from the masters, Brahms, Schubert, Strauss and Tschaikovsky.

All of the dances have been successfully taught to a group of students in my own school. The correlated material has also been used by them with a rare sense of understanding and appreciation. Dances in this collection have been given on programs at University of Georgia, Music Appreciation Series; Brenau College; Coordinate College, University of Georgia; Lucy Cobb Chapel for six consecutive years; Georgia State D. A. R. Convention; Georgia State Nurses Association; Georgia Dance Conference at Camp Chattooga; Lunar Club, College of Agriculture; and Athens High School P.T.A.

The welfare of each individual student has always been foremost. If a sacrifice must be made, it is always the program, rather than the child. Children in the school are never forced to do dances. Compositions are especially composed to meet the varied physical abilities and art interests of each student. Consequently, they enter into their dancing with great vigor and enthusiasm. The creative spirit is at all times fostered and the children are encouraged under careful supervision to compose their own dances. The material is graded according to age and development of the student (see educational chart in Dance Section), and both content and form are unified to give artistic significance to each composition. It is earnestly hoped that this method will prove a source of inspiration to other teachers and students as they work together to create harmony and beauty for the children of the people.

I wish to express my gratitude to the following artists for their understanding cooperation: to Harriet W. Frishmuth for permission to use "Crest of the Wave", "Desha" and "The Dancers" and also for very beautiful photographs of these sculptures; to Maude Jewett for permission to use "The Flower Holder"; to Bonnie MacLeary for "Aspiration"; to Bessie Potter Vonnoh for "L'Allegresse"; to Edwin Markham for permission to quote the line, "Come, let us live the poetry we sing" from "The Desire of Nations"; to Marjorie Allen Seiffert for "They Who Dance"; to Ruth St. Denis for "Dancers of the New Age"; to Amanda Benjamin Hall for "The Dancer in the Shrine"; to Dr. William Norman Guthrie for "The Hymn of Jesus"; to Bernice Oehler for her sketches of Lucile Marsh and Ruth St. Denis; to Dr. Tait McKenzie for "The Joy of Effort"; to Malvina Hoffman for "Autumn Bacchanale"; to Mario Korbel for "The Three Graces"; to Frances Grimes for the reliefs, "Girl Dancing"; to Wheeler Williams for "The Three Graces"; to Alexander Oppler for "Pavlowa" by Ernst Oppler; to Troy Kinney for "La Gavotte Pavlowa" and "Les Sylphides"; to Boris Blai for "Mary Wigman," and to John Cowper Powys for the poem, "To Isadora Duncan."

My hearty thanks are proffered the following museums for their assistance with photographs of masterpieces: to the Metropolitan Museum of Art for "Connie Gilchrist" by Whistler, "Aspiration" by MacLeary, "Andante" by Korbel, "Pavlowa" by Lenz, "Rehearsal on the Stage" by Degas, "Slavonic Dance" by Frishmuth, "Neo-Attic Marble Vase" and "French XVIII Century Panels"; to The Detroit Institute of Arts for "L'Allegresse" by Bessie Potter Vonnoh; to The Art Institute of Chicago for "The Dancing Lesson" by Cecilia Beaux, and "Dancer and Gazelles" by Paul Manship; to The Isabella Stewart Gardner Museum, Boston, for "El Jaleo" by Sargent; to the City Art Museum, St. Louis, for "Betalo Rubino" by Robert Henri; to Mr. Joseph Widener for "The Young Dancer" by Renoir; to the A. W. Mellon Educational Trust and the Duveen Bros. for "La Camargo" by Lancret; to the Prado Museum, Madrid, for "Peasant Dance" by Rubens; and to the Louvre, Paris, for "La Danse" by Carpeaux.

My appreciation is also extended to the following publishers, who granted permission to reprint poems: to the McMillan Company for "Dance, My Heart!" from "Songs of Kabir" by Rabindranath Tagore, "Barter" from "Love Songs" by Sara Teasdale and "The Dance" from "Youth Riding" by Mary Carolyn Davies; to Brandt and Brandt for the sonnet on the dance by Edna St. Vincent Millay; to Dodd, Mead and Co. for "To Leilehua" by Don Blanding; to E. P. Dutton and Co. for the lines, "Soul and body are alike divine and the soul grows like a flower on the body's stem" from "Gods Who Dance" by Ted Shawn; to Alfred A. Knopf for "The Dancer" from "The Wanderer—His Parables and Sayings" by Kahlil Gibran; to Contemporary Verse for the poem, "To Dance", by Margaret B. McGee; to the Turner Co. for "The Day" from "Songs for Courage" by Grace Noll Crowell; to the Century Magazine for "The Joy of Effort" by Charles Wharton Stork; to The American Dancer Magazine for "Mary Wigman", "A Glad Surrender", "Behold! I Dance My Faith!" and "When I Dance Statues"; to The Foreword of the Three Arts Club for "Dance Realization" and "A Cup of Joy"; to Theater Arts for "Pavlowa Crossed the Stage" by Charles Ballard; to Houghton-Mifflin Co. for "Dancers of the New Age" from "Lotus Light" by Ruth St. Denis.

I also wish to thank Mr. William Drake of the Gorham Company for his contribution of photographs of "The Crescent Moon" and "Desha" by Harriet Frishmuth and "The Flower Holder" by Maude Jewett; and Curtis and Cameron Company for the photograph of "Pavanne" by Sir Edwin Austin Abbey.

Lines from Byron are from "Monody on the Death of the Rt. Hon. R. B. Sheridan."

Lines from Michael Angelo's sonnet are from Mrs. Henry Roscoe's translation.

Lines from Shakespeare are from "The Winter's Tale"—Florizel's speech in regard to the dancing Perdita.

Lines, "Body and soul are alike divine and the soul grows like a flower on the body's stem" are quoted from W. B. Seabrook's interview with a tribe of dancing Dervishes in "Gods Who Dance" by Ted Shawn.

I wish to express my heartfelt thanks to Lucile Marsh for many helpful suggestions in revising the manuscript, to Elizabeth Allgood Birchmore for her gracious assistance in helping to harmonize the dance with music, to Margarethe Morris Parrott for transposing the Schubert Ecossaisen and to Mr. L. C. Arnett and Mr. H. G. Gates for photographic studies of the dances.

I also wish my students to know that their love of the dance and their devotion have been constant sources of inspiration to me.

LUCY LAMPKIN
January, 1936

The Cover

THE cover for "The Dance in Art" is symbolic. Blue is the color of the water and the sky. It gives a sense of space. Blue has an ethereal quality. As used in the medieval religious paintings, it is the color of faith.

Blue, as a color, expresses the aspirations of the soul of man. It is said that a certain group of young Brahmin priests of Japan, followed by the boys in their charge, ascend a high hill each morning. Standing here, surrounded by beauty, they say, "Blue water, blue sky, blue mountains and I." Then, standing firmly on the earth, they reach up to the sky.

Silver gives a sense of illumination. Here, it symbolizes the celebration of the joy and beauty of life, which is the message of the artist.

The five straight-lined spaces represent the five arts: Painting, Poetry, Sculpture, Music and Dancing. The two triangles which if extended would form one large triangle, represent aspiration, the dominant quality of the dedicated artist. The large middle space represents a "Door to Life," lived in beauty, harmony and proportion. The small inner circle represents the Heart of the Universe, the Creative Whole, from which all things radiate. The two semi-circles represent an echo of this greater creative whole of which the artist has a share. The large circle represents the love of beauty which binds all people together. The design, as a whole, is intended to give a feeling of going forward and reaching upward.

It is the eternal seeking the gods adore!

L. L.

Contents

Contents

List of Illustrations

List of Illustrations

Foreword

THIS book with its fine spirit of aspiration towards Eternal Beauty with its poems and pictures selected with taste and understanding seems to me to be a real contribution to the Dance.

The Dance of to-day in America is caught between the upper and the nether millstones of a commercial age on one side, and the yearning of the soul and body to reveal itself in the splendors of rhythm, form and color. We stand on the threshold of new visions and new articulations of the Dance, but its real progress lies ever in the hands of those who hold it as the possible super language of the expanding spirit of humanity. This I am sure, Miss Lampkin does and I wish her a grateful and sympathetic public for the beauty she has wrought in her book.

RUTH ST. DENIS

Introduction

IN the Middle Ages beautiful paintings and sculpture were collected by the monarchs to adorn their palaces. The leading artists worked under royal command and protection. Art belonged to the nobility. The Dance which was once the joyous expression of the Folk became the artistic expression of a professional group. Under the refinement of court influence it lost the spontaneity and freedom of movement which gave it birth. Poetry, too, became the instrument of expression of the court bards. With the development of opera and the symphony Music became so highly sublimated that a cultural background was necessary to completely understand and appreciate it. Even Drama, which was an integral part of worship in the Miracle and Mystery Plays, became the means of expression of a small group of professional actors.

But art no longer belongs to the "chosen few." To-day, we have the great museums open to the masses for pleasure and instruction. New York, alone, has a number, including: the Metropolitan, the Roerich, the Whitney Museum of American Art, the Museum of Modern Art and the Grand Central Art Gallery which exhibits the works of living American sculptors and painters. Clay modeling and painting are being taught in the schools and colleges. In the field of Drama, we have the Theater Guild and Eva Le Gallienne's Civic Repertory Theater of New York and the Little Theater Movement, which has rapidly spread throughout the country. Hugh Mearns has conducted a marvelously successful experiment in the creative writing of Poetry. His book, "Creative Youth," contains gems of poetic expression from young writers. Each year adds a new name to the long list of poetry magazines. Walter Damrosch with his symphony concerts over radio and his wonderful educational programs for the public schools, is making music a feast for all the children in the land.

In the Renaissance of the Dance, those two pioneers and prophets, Isadora Duncan and Ruth St. Denis blazed the trail for other feet to follow. At the present time, there are many schools of real artistic value. In the large cities, there are concert dancers of skill and dedication, while in the small towns, there are groups, working with eagerness and devotion. Lucile Marsh, with rare genius and insight, has brought the Dance to the schools and colleges, where it is rapidly becoming an educational device of proven merit. Margaret H'Doubler has caused the Dance to receive high academic recognition at the University of Wisconsin where a Master's Degree is given in the art. Phoebe Guthrie has given back to the Dance its rightful place in the church. At St. Mark's in-the-Bouwerie in New York she and her group have performed dances of great spiritual beauty.

The arts are related just as the sciences are related. The great artists of the world have seen this relationship and many of them have become skilled in more than one art. A love and understanding of one art will lead to an appreciation of all the arts, because the same fundamental principles apply to each and every one.

But, Life is infinitely greater and more significant than art, and only as the artist holds this concept in mind, will his works be inspiring and his values clear. We have built our museums and art centers and now we must look to the building of our bodies. We must give to the new generation all the beauty and spirituality which they so hunger for and which they are so capable of expressing. We must make our bodies living sculpture; our movements, those of a beautiful dance; our voices, instruments of harmonious musical expression; our speech, the rhythmic cadence of the greatest poems; our houses and our clothes, the symphonies of color found in the paintings of the masters; and our actions, those of the deep and inspired moments of the greatest dramas.

No one can study or practice an art without realizing the age-old truth, "As we live, so do we grow." As we think and feel, so will we grow spiritually; as we move, so will we grow physically. Every child has a right to the heritage of beauty expressed in the arts. The Dance should be a part of every child's education to insure the development of beautiful bodies during the entire period of growth and to give the joyous experience of vigorous and spirited movement to the Music of the Masters. Beautiful movement inspires beautiful thought and so we have a never-ending circle of growth in beauty which is the most inspired goal in the training of children. In this age of art cults, here are treasures which will endure from one generation to another.

Art appeals to the emotions, and it is through art that the emotions may be schooled in beauty of expression. The Dance becomes for the dancer so personal that this beauty when practiced becomes a part of his own personality. Art becomes a vital glow; beauty becomes a thing we humans can touch and live. The great dancers of the world have spoken to frail and superficial humanity in the language of movement. When a radiant and beautiful personality speaks through movement, the world is silent. When a perfect body is the external expression of an inner spiritual quality, the world gazes in reverent awe and admiration.

Part I

Poems of the Dance

LUCILE MARSH

Come, let us live the poetry we sing.

EDWIN MARKHAM

The Dancer

Once there came to the court of the Prince of Birkasha a dancer with her musicians. And she was admitted to the court, and she danced before the prince to the music of the lute and the flute and the zither.

She danced the dance of flames, and the dance of swords and spears; she danced the dance of stars and the dance of space. And then she danced the dance of flowers in the wind.

After this she stood before the throne of the prince and bowed her body before him. And the prince bade her to come nearer, and he said unto her, "Beautiful woman, daughter of grace and delight, whence comes your art? And how is it that you command all the elements in your rhythms and your rhymes?"

And the dancer bowed again before the prince, and she answered, "Mighty and gracious Majesty, I know not the answer to your questionings. Only this I know: The philosopher's soul dwells in his head; the poet's soul is in his heart; the singer's soul lingers about his throat, but the soul of the dancer abides in all her body."

From "The Wanderer
His Parables and Sayings"
By KAHLIL GIBRAN

Behold! I Dance My Faith!

Behold!   I dance my faith!

Faith in the beauty of living,
The changing color of days
That come with a golden splendor
And go in a coral blaze.

Faith in the chosen task,
Courageously begun
And years upon years of labor,
For a goal is not easily won.

Faith in the glory of moving
With a rhythm as strong and free
As the recurrent rise and fall
Of waves on a wind-swept sea.

Faith in the joy of giving,
Constantly without end,
As ripened fruit bows down the tree
And the heavy branches bend.

Faith in the growth of all things—
The steady advancing beat
Of music that surges and sings
And children's dancing feet.

Faith in the soul's deep yearning
And a climb to the highest hill,
When the ancient stars are shining
And the valley lies hushed and still.

L. L.

The Dancer in the Shrine

I am a dancer. When I pray
I do not gather thoughts with clumsy thread
Into poor phrases. Birds all have a way
Of singing home the truth that they are birds,
And so my loving litany is said
Without the aid of words.
I am a dancer. Under me
The floor gleams lapis lazuli,
With inlaid gems of every hue—
Mother o' pearl I tread like dew,
While at the window of her frame
Our Lady, of the hallowed name,
Leans on the sill. Grey saints glare down,
Too long by godliness entranced,
With piety of painted frown,
Who never danced—
But Oh, Our Lady's quaint, arrested look
Remembers when she danced with bird and brook,
Of wind and flower and innocence a part,
Before the rose of Jesus kissed her heart
And men heaped heavy prayers upon her breast.
She watches me with gladness half confessed
Who dare to gesture homage with my feet
Or twinkle lacy steps of joy
To entertain the Holy Boy;
Who, laughing, pirouette and pass,
Translated by the colored glass,
To meanings infinitely sweet.
And though it is not much, I know,
To fan the incense to and fro
With skirt as flighty as a wing,
It seems Our Lady understands
The method of my worshipping,
The hymns I'm lifting in my hands—
I am a dancer—

AMANDA BENJAMIN HALL

[5]

The Hymn of Jesus

(Based on a fourth century poem)

When ye dance (saith the Lord)
Ye shall yield up yourselves wholly
That the Spirit may take possession;
For it sweepeth you on afar
And lifteth you aloft,
Till ye mount above the world
And float and rest in Heaven,—
Even as I, your Lord.

They that will not dance
Forever shall know not
What the children of God now are knowing.

Fain would I move to you,
O music of holy souls.

Dr. William Norman Guthrie

("The Hymn of Jesus" is not only a surviving specimen of early rituals in honor of our Lord; it is itself the climax of a "dromenon" or sacred drama. All early cults conveyed their meaning to their initiates through a dance, enacting a myth-nucleus, that is, a "dromenon." The Religious Dance should always be "an oblation of the Human Body to the Holy Spirit of God", as devoutly aware as possible of an everlasting self-renewal of man by the continuous incarnation of the Divine Ideal.)

From leaflet, St. Mark's in-the-Bouwerie

The Dance

God's in me when I dance
God, making Spring
Out of His thoughts
And building worlds
By wishing.
God
Laughing at His own
Queer fancies,
Standing awed,
And sobbing;
Musing,
Dreaming,
Throbbing;
Commanding;
Creating—
God's in me
When I dance.

MARY CAROLYN DAVIES

Pavlowa Crossed the Stage

Pavlowa crossed the stage;
　Who heard her go?
A bird might pass at dusk
　Even so.

Does a song touch the ground,
　Gliding over?
Does a butterfly bend
　The red clover?

I could not hear her pass,
　Nor could you.
Who hears a summer cloud
　Cross the blue?

She is gone, but dreaming still,
　I see her go.
Would I could walk the earth
　Even so!

Charles Ballard

To Isadora Duncan

With the gesture of a god,
You gave me back my youth,
And a scent of violets
Overflowed the world.
With the gesture of a god,
You gave me back my love,
And tears deeper than tears
Overflowed my heart.
With the gesture of a god,
You trampled on fate,
You lifted up on high
Those that had fallen—
All the oppressed,
All the humiliated,
All the offended;
You lifted them up on high
And they were comforted.
With the gesture of a god,
You wrestled with Demogorgon;
You brought hope back
And freedom and triumph
To those whom the world had crushed.
All of us, sitting in darkness,
Saw a great light—
You danced as dance the morning stars
And the universe was conquered.

JOHN COWPER POWYS

Dancers of the New Age

We are the dancers of the new age!
The revealers of the glory that has been shown,
The prophets of the glory that is to come.

Within the temple of the dance
We have become as priests of the new day,
And perform our mighty ritual of beauty.

Only obedience to law is liberty,
But that liberty is beauty,
And that law divine.

Hidden from dull ears and veiled from blinded eyes
Is the great rhythm of the universe,
And we are the rhythms of the law made visible.

We bring to you proportion, which is order,
Rhythm, which is power,
And beauty, which is joy.

Behold the vision of your greater selves,
The images of your dreams,
Dancing upon the mountains.

O World,
Behold and live again,
We have found the secret,
We have found the way,

It is to dance!

RUTH ST. DENIS

Reprinted from "Lotus Light" by permission of Houghton Mifflin Company

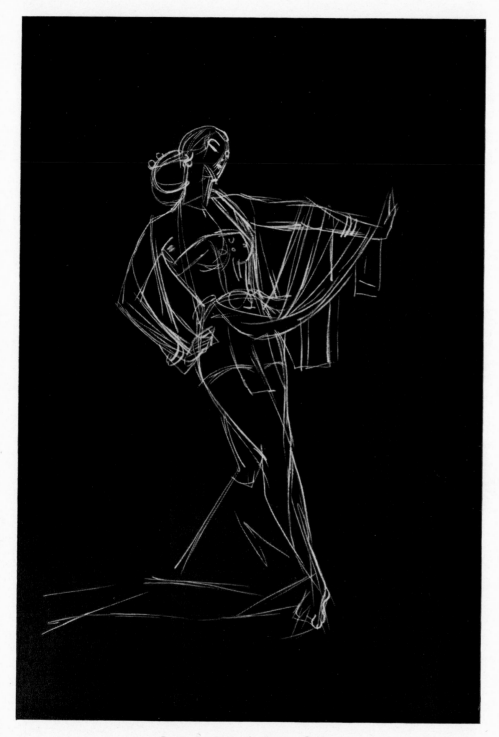

Ruth St. Denis by Bernice Oehler

To Leilehua

(Who caught the poetry of Hawaii in her hula-dance)

Swift-changing curves. The gestures of her hands
Taught waves to draw white lines upon the sands.

Slim fingers, tipped like gulls' wings bent in flight;
Dark tropic eyes, deep sky-black pools of night.

Slow fluid curves. A body young and gay . . .
A flower watched her dance and learned to sway.

From throat to wrist . . . sweet slipping wilting lines
That stole their grace from wind-waved mai-le vines.

Her dance, a mystic half-forgotten rite
Before some Polynesian god at night.

Don Blanding

Dance Realization

I dance with complete abandon
I pour forth my spirit
In the ecstasy of rhythm,
The movements of my body
Are free and sure.
My dance is one of naked strength;
I dance
A promise of fulfillment—
The great chords
Of Life's Symphony
Are sounding nearer and nearer
And I know that I shall become
What I believe!

L. L.

Mary Wigman

I have a banner to hold;
I shall fling it high
And carry it, a black torch
Against the sky.

Dauntless it streaks,
Not brightly hued, not white,
But as black smoke coils
Against the tarnished night.

Now soars to a plaintive song,
Resounds a shouting dirge,
The depths of a thousand voices
To silence and purge.

I hold a funeral mantle;
I hold a battle cry
To fling against the tawdry world
And watch the splintered ashes fly.

FRANCES FORBES

A Glad Surrender

Give yourself to joy, bending,
Curving in a glad surrender,
Yielding to her rays of light,
Like a candle, white and slender.
Be fleet of foot
And you will catch her in a race;
Fling yourself to Joy
And Joy will send you laughing into space.
Come, seek the path of Joy
And you will find the mark
Of sandaled feet that dance
A rhythmic pattern through the dark.
Reach high up for Joy;
Stretch out your hands in mirth
And other hands will meet to dance
A radiant circle round the earth!

L. L.

Portrait of Isadora

A radiant figure dancing,
Clad in brilliant hue;
A starry-eyed madonna,
Wrapped in a robe of blue.

A Grecian maiden bearing
A garland to her shrine;
A wild bacchante whirling,
Caught up by heady wine.

A dance in a dim cathedral
By mellow candle-light,
The glow of crimson roses
On an altar gleaming white.

A curving fluid movement
To music that surges and sings,
A spirit of flame and shadow,
Borne up on luminous wings.

A shout for a wider freedom,
A long lost battle-cry,
A fearless leader fighting
For a cause that will not die.

A funeral march and war-cry,
A challenge and a song;
Then a long low sigh as plaintive
As a note on an Eastern gong.

A mystic compelling beauty,
A face turned toward the light,
Arms lifted in supplication,
Eyes fixed on a distant height.

A radiant figure dancing,
Clad in brilliant hue;
A starry-eyed madonna,
Wrapped in a robe of blue.

L. L.

They Who Dance

The feet of dancers
Shine with laughter,
Their hearts are vibrant as bells;

The air flows by them
Divided, like water
Before a gleaming ship.

Triumphantly their bodies sing,
Their eyes
Are blind with music.

They move through threatening ghosts,
Feeling them as cool as mist
Against their brows.

They who dance
Find infinite golden floors
Beneath their feet.

Marjorie Allen Seiffert

To Dance

I want to dance!
When the sun catches the aspen leaves
They dance;
When it flecks the grasses and mottles the streams
They dance;
When the dark storm bends the black branches
And the wind whips up the waves
They dance;
The bird swings on the elm twig,
The sap races in the tree,
Horses run in the pasture,
Mist fairies glide to and fro in the valley,
Cloud children play in heaven,
The stars sing and dance,
And I want to dance!
I can be rain-drops.
I can be leaves and bending grasses,
Gold mottled streams and running horses,
Racing sap and the hidden heart of flowers.
I can be fire light and moon light,
A child of the night mist and a sister of the stars.
All the world sings and dances,
And I am a child of all the world. I want to sing, and—
I want to dance.

Margaret B. McGee

Sonnet

How healthily their feet upon the floor
Strike down!—These are no spirits, but a band
Of children, surely, leaping hand in hand
Into the air in groups of three and four,
Wearing their silken rags as if they wore
Leaves only and light grasses, or a strand
Of black, elusive seaweed oozing sand,
And running hard as if along a shore.
I know how lost forever, and at length
How still, these lovely tossing limbs shall lie,
And the bright laughter and the panting breath,
And yet, before such beauty and such strength,
Once more, as always when the dance is high,
I am rebuked that I believe in death.

Edna St. Vincent Millay

Dance, My Heart!

Dance, my heart! Dance today with joy.

The strains of love fill the days and the nights with music, and the world
    is listening to its melodies:

Mad with joy, life and death dance to the rhythm of this music. The hills
    and the sea and the earth dance.
The world of man dances in laughter and tears.

Why put on the robe of the monk, and live aloof from the world in lonely
    pride?
Behold! my heart dances in the delight of a hundred arts; and the Creator
    is well pleased.

RABINDRANATH TAGORE

The Joy of Effort

(Sonnet inspired by R. Tait McKenzie's medallion, "The Joy of Effort", representing the flight of three hurdlers. The original medallion is placed in the wall of the stadium at Stockholm to commemorate the Olympic Games of 1912.)

Eager as fire, impetuous as the wind,
    They spurn the ground and lightly clear the bar,
Three racers? Nay, three strong wills unconfined,
    Three glad, contending swiftnesses they are:
  Three dolphins that with simultaneous leap
    Breast the high breaker of a tropic surge,
As flashing silvery from the purple deep
    And scattering foam, their curving backs emerge;
Three agile swallows, skimming near the ground
    That give their bodies to the buoyant air;
Three roebucks fleet that through the forest bound.
    Yet how can even such with men compare?
Not with mere pride of strength are these alive;
    The noblest joy of being is to strive.

CHARLES WHARTON STORK

© "THE JOY OF EFFORT" by R. Tait McKenzie

Part II

Paintings of the Dance

The glowing portraits, fresh from life, that bring
Home to our hearts the truths from which they spring

BYRON

"Peasant Dance" by Rubens

"La Camargo" by Nicolas Lancret

Degas
Rehearsal on the stage

"The Young Dancer" by Renoir

You belong to a world aloof,
A world of tinsel and lace;
Yet the wisdom of all the ages
Shines out from your lovely face.

L. L.

Anna Pavlowa

"The Dying Swan" by Ernst Oppler

"THE DANCING LESSON" by Cecilia Beaux

Together we dance, my child;
Your feet are eager to learn,
For you are caught up into Life
And I into Love!

L. L.

"CONNIE GILCHRIST" by J. A. McNeill Whistler

Whistler has caught your beauty
And held it for all to see.
Your beauty belongs to a dancer;
Your picture, to me!

L. L.

© "Pavanne" by Sir Edwin Austin Abbey

[41]

Courtesy of the City Art Museum, St. Louis

BETALO RUBINO—"Dramatic Dancer" by Robert Henri

"El Jaleo" by John Singer Sargent   *Courtesy of The Gardner Museum, Boston*

Bright hands clapping, light feet tapping;
    Rhythm fills the air.
Red lips smiling, eyes beguiling,
    Color everywhere!

Lamps are gleaming, faces beaming;
    The dancer taps her heel.
Eyes are glowing, rapture knowing,
    The Pride of old Seville!

                L. L.

Troy Kinney

La Gavotte Pavlowa

LES SYLPHIDES—Lopokova and Nijinsky

[49]

Part III

Sculptures of the Dance

The stone unhewn and cold
Becomes a living mold,
The more the marble wastes
The more the statue grows.

Michael Angelo

Roman Period

NEO-ATTIC MARBLE VASE

I Century B.C.—I Century A.D.

French XVIII Century Panels

Ormolu figures on wood

[55]

"La Danse" by Carpeaux

First Section of Frieze Panels, bas-relief, PAVLOWA and MORDKIN
in "AUTUMN BACCHANALE," by Malvina Hoffman

Come, drink of the wine of the god
And catch me in fond embrace,
For the hours are fleeting away
And Life is a keen, swift race.

L. L.

[59]

Courtesy of The Metropolitan Museum of Art

"Pavlowa" by Alfred Lenz

What rapture sent you soaring high,
  What magic held you there?
What visions of your loveliness
  Are with us everywhere!

L. L.

"Aspiration" by Bonnie MacLeary

Out of a mist—the blue!
Out of the dusk—a glow!
From infinite longing—to know:
The goal is never won,
The task is just begun;
It is the eternal seeking
    The gods adore!

                L. L.

"ANDANTE" by Joseph Mario Korbel

So fair young bodies dance a hymn of praise
To worship Nature's God and Nature's Self.

L. L.

"SLAVONIC DANCE" by Harriet W. Frishmuth

"Three Graces" or "Rhythm of the Waves" by Wheeler Williams
(Based on Isadora Duncan's dance and posed by three of the Duncan Dancers)

[69]

"THREE GRACES" by Joseph Mario Korbel
(Based on Isadora Duncan's dance)

Courtesy of Miss Grimes
Photograph by de Witt Ward

"GIRL DANCING" by Frances Grimes

"GIRL DANCING" by Frances Grimes

© "L'Allegresse" by Bessie Potter Vonnoh

Weaving in and out they come,
They balance and retreat;
Perfect rapture of the dance,
They feel in rhythmic beat!

L. L.

"MARY WIGMAN" by Boris Blai

"Dancer and Gazelles" by Paul Manship

© "Desha" by Harriet W. Frishmuth

A perfect form imbued with grace,
A singing balance caught in place!

L. L.

© "The Flower Holder" by Maude S. Jewett

"Soul and body are alike divine
and
The soul grows like a flower
on
The body's stem."

[85]

© "The Crescent Moon" by Grace Talbot

How slowly she glides and softly!
She curves a misty veil over the moon.
Her hands are like fragile petals;
Her body, a delicate flower of June.

L. L.

[87]

© "Crest of the Wave" by Harriet W. Frishmuth

When you do dance, I wish you
A wave o' the sea, that might ever do
Nothing but that; move still, still so,
And own no other function.

SHAKESPEARE

[89]

"The Dancers" by Harriet W. Frishmuth

Dance on forever and ever!
Be gay and strong and free.
The Joy of Life is calling you;
Dance on in ecstasy!

L. L.

Part IV

Twelve Dances with Music

In all its best periods the dance has flourished in a luxurious background of other arts. Through the ages, poets, sculptors, painters, and musicians have derived some of their finest inspiration from Terpsichore. In turn, her artists have been stimulated and sustained in their creative work by masterpieces from other fields of art.

Since learning is merely a recapitulation of the evolution of an art, it is not surprising that students of the dance master their art most quickly and completely when it is presented in its natural setting of the fine arts. In fact, to attempt to present the dance without its origins in the culture, art, and philosophy of civilization is as futile as to attempt to cultivate flowers without their roots.

The intrinsic beauty, vitality, and individuality of an art is always better proven by juxtaposition than by isolation, and great artists of all times have been able to give and take without jeopardizing the essential integrity of their own art.

Lucile Marsh

Educational Analysis

Dance	Grade	Idea	Emotion	Body Skills	Movements	Art Principles
"Three Graces"	H.S.	Sculpture	Faith, Hope, Love	Balance Lightness	Waltz Balancing Turning	Harmony Variety
"Lullaby"	Kindergarten	Lullaby Song	Gentleness Tenderness	Balance Relaxation	Balancing Turning	Unity; Variety Detail
"Two Little Colonels"	Kindergarten I	Book, Movie	Joy, Pride Loyalty	Lightness Daintiness	Sliding, Pointing, Polka	Rhythm Bisymmetry
"Playing Statue"	III-VI	"Statues" Poem	Joy, Aspiration Determination	Precision Balance	Skipping Sitting Standing	Form Harmony
"Gossip"	J.H.	Poem	Humor Gayety	Imitation Minute Gestures	Nodding Head Shaking Hands Walking	Rhythm Motivation
"Mazurka"	J.H.	Folk Dance	Vivacity Abandon	Speed Strength	Mazurka Step Turn and Stamp Lunging	Contrast Variety Rhythm
"At the Museum"	J.H.	Sculpture Poem	Appreciation Wonder Joy	Balance Precision	Sculpture Transitions	Form, Harmony Design
"Joy" Dance-Poem	III	"Joy" Poem	Joy Generosity	Balance Transition	Rising Turning Running	Design Motivation Symmetry
"Play"	III-VI	Play	Joy, Humor Surprise	Transition Lightness Speed	Leaping Running Turning	Motivation Rhythm Design
"March"	H.S.	March in Geometric Patterns	None Mechanical	Accuracy Strength Precision	Walking Lunging	Composition Form Design
"Dance of Banners"	J.H.	Poem	Courage Leadership Dedication	Strength Control Endurance	Leaping Lunging Falling	Enlargement Climax
"The Day"	H.S.	Poem	Contemplation of Beauty Ecstasy	Precision Transition	Rising Walking Turning Arabesque	Crescendo Diminuendo Form Contrast

Stage Directions

Back Drop

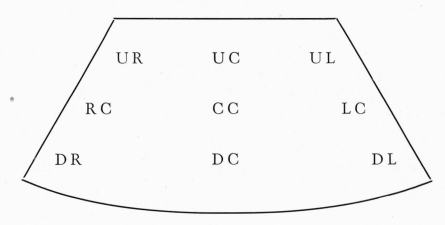

Audience

Symbols

U—Up stage, to the back of stage or away from audience
D—Down stage, to the front of stage or toward audience
L—Left, dancer's left when she faces audience
R—Right, dancer's right when she faces audience
C—Center of stage from left to right or from up to down
C C—Center of stage from left to right and from up to down
D L—Down left, etc.
S—Stage

Photography by Gates

The Three Graces

The Three Graces

Dedicated to "Dance Art Group."

A dance for six girls, ages 12-14, based on famous sculptures of the "Three Graces" (Faith, Hope and Love).

Show the children the sculpture photographs in Sculpture Section, before teaching the dance.

Costume:—Flesh chiffon classic drapery to ankles, slit about 14 inches up from bottom at seam on each side to give freedom of movement and held with two elastics, one at breasts, the other below hips at bottom of leotard.

Music:—Strauss Waltz—"Thousand and One Nights."

I   See sculpture by Korbel "The Three Graces," page 71. Three girls (3 each side U S) take positions of this famous sculpture.

Theme A

(a) All double balance forward and back 2 (meas. 1-4) - - - - - 4 meas.
Central figure whirl in place and 2 side figures balance toward and away from central figure (meas. 5-8) - - - - - - - 4 meas.

(b) Central figure now changes hands and touches finger tips of her own hands together in circle overhead 1 hand palm down, one palm up.
2 side figures have inside arms held out toward central figure and outside arms curved upward.
All waltz forward with tiny steps and hold (meas. 9-16) - - - 8 meas.

II   All dance in circle to R with:—
Step-slide-close-flying turn   Repeat theme A
(Step R-slide-close L pivot R, turning completely around with L lifted off floor.)
On flying turn, have finger tips touching in circle, 1 hand palm down, other palm up and swing arms to R.
7 turns and hold (meas. 1-14) - - - - - - - - - - 14 meas.
Whirl in place (meas. 15-16) - - - - - - - - - - 2 meas.

_____

Finish U C, 2 groups having exchanged places - - - - - - 16 meas.

III (a) All join hands in line formation U C   Theme B
Waltz forward with:—
Step-swing-step-close (2 meas.)
Repeat 7 times and finish D C - - - - - - - - - 16 meas.

(b) Waltz in 2 lines, passing each other, each dancing in semi-circle to U C.

Each group of 3 then waltzes around in small circle and ends in line formation.

Waltz here is:—Step R-slide-L-close R ⸳ ⸳ ⸳ ⸳ ⸳ ⸳ Repeat   16 meas.

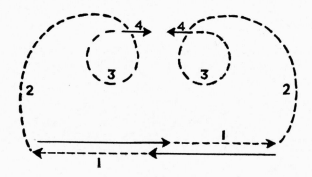

IV (a) See sculpture of "Allegresse" by Bessie Potter Vonnoh, page 77.
Two groups of 3 take position of "Allegresse".
Girl on R of central figure make complete turn toward central figure and waltz 2 in place ⸳ ⸳ ⸳ ⸳ ⸳ ⸳ ⸳ ⸳ ⸳ ⸳ (1-4)   4 meas.
Girl on L of central figure make complete turn away from central figure and waltz 2 in place ⸳ ⸳ ⸳ ⸳ ⸳ ⸳ ⸳ ⸳ ⸳ (5-8)   4 meas.
Central figure whirl in place (2 meas.)
Hold 2 meas. ⸳ ⸳ ⸳ ⸳ ⸳ ⸳ ⸳ ⸳ ⸳ ⸳ ⸳ ⸳ (9-12)   4 meas.
All hold in place 2 meas.
All whirl and take position of "Three Graces" by Germain Pilon 2 meas. ⸳ ⸳ ⸳ ⸳ ⸳ ⸳ ⸳ ⸳ ⸳ ⸳ ⸳ (13-16)   4 meas.

————————

16 meas.

(This may be purchased in post card form from The Art Museum of Chicago)
Position is:—Three figures standing close together, back to back, central figure facing forward, 2 side figures facing outward. All have arms down, hands touching and one knee bent.

(b) Pilon Figure:—
All take double balance forward and back with tiny steps. Take 2 little step-draws to R, making a half-turn ⸳ ⸳ ⸳ ⸳ (17-20)   4 meas.
Repeat, finishing turn ⸳ ⸳ ⸳ ⸳ ⸳ ⸳ ⸳ ⸳ ⸳ (20-24)   4 meas.

(c) Separate (Arms in Greek fifth, curved overhead, one hand under the other)
2 front figures waltz forward—
2 inside figures waltz toward each other, and 1 clasps arms around waist of other, whose arms are circled upward in Greek fifth. Both waltz turn.

2 outside figures waltz turn in place, arms in Greek 5th   (25-28)   4 meas.

o o——→ ←——o o

   o   o

   | |

   ↓   ↓

All waltz back to original places (29-32) · · · · · · · · · 4 meas.

V   (a) Two groups of 3 in circle (back to back) hands joined and arms raised. (Position of "Bronze Flower Holder" by E. Angela, Gorham Co.) All single balance forward and back, enlarging movement with swing.
Leaning to R, hands still joined, all run in circle to R.
Finish, facing in · · · · · · · · · · · (meas. 1-8) 8 meas.

   (b) Repeat balance and run, facing in (9-16) · · · · · · · · 8 meas.
Finish in straight line, facing forward.

VI   Two groups of three dance on diagonal, 1 group to R, 1 group to L. Begin with 2 groups U S

   (a) Directions for group U R; other group opposite.
Lean forward and circle R arm over and touch fingers to back of L hand, R knee bent.
Lift R arm up and back, at same time, swing R leg forward and lean back. (2 meas.)
Run forward (2 meas.) and whirl in place (4 meas.) (meas. 17-24) 8 meas.

   (b) Repeat same movements and dance back to place (meas. 25-32) 8 meas.

VII   All six in line formation, arms around waists.

   (a) Bend forward and back (remember to push hips forward and lift arches and ankles).
Run forward and whirl separately · · · · · (meas. 17-24) 8 meas.

   (b) Bend forward and back and run back to place.
Take position of "Three Graces" by Wheeler Williams, page 69
                                 (25-32) 8 meas.

VIII   In this position, balance forward and back 2.

   (a) Waltz forward (1-8) · · · · · · · · · · · · · · · 8 meas.
Balance forward and back 2 and waltz back (9-16) · · · · · 8 meas.

   (b) All take position of "Danseuses Borghese" from the Louvre.
Position is:—Line formation, hands joined, every other girl face in and out.

All waltz in this position in line circling from R to L and L to R
as in diagram (17-32) ` ` ` ` ` ` ` ` ` ` ` ` ` ` 16 meas.

Finish D S C.

(c) Two groups of three join R hands and run around very fast with
dipping motion (32-39) ` ` ` ` ` ` ` ` ` ` ` ` ` ` 8 meas.

Three groups of two (1 girl—arms in Greek 5th, other girl—arms
around waist of 1st)

All whirl very fast around and hold (40-48) ` ` ` ` ` ` ` 8 meas.

The Three Graces

"Three Graces"—Korbel

J. STRAUSS, Op. 346

(a) "ALLEGRESSE"- Vonnoh

(b) "THREE GRACES"- Pilon

[104]

"THREE GRACES"

"THREE GRACES"– Williams

"DANSEUSES BORGHESE"

[106]

Photography by Gates

LULLABY

Lullaby

Music—Brahms Lullaby—Omit introduction
Play once and repeat

(For children 4-6. The famous Brahms Lullaby is sung by a young girl as accompaniment for the dance. The children are costumed in Leotards, over which is worn a sky blue china silk tunic, draped according to classic lines and coming above the knee. Very little children may wear a sash of the same material. The singer wears a long white dress and a Madonna blue satin robe, made also on classic lines and trailing the floor in back.)

(Many translations are given of this German song. We used the following and took the liberty of singing the first verse last and the second verse first, as written.)

> "Lullaby and Good Night,
> Thy mother's delight,
> Bright angels around
> My darling shall stand;
> They will guard thee from harms,
> Thou shalt wake in my arms.
> They will guard thee from harms,
> Thou shalt wake in my arms.
>
> Lullaby and Good Night,
> With roses bedight,
> With lilies bespread
> Is baby's wee bed.
> Lay thee down now and rest,
> May thy slumber be blest.
> Lay thee down now and rest,
> May thy slumber be blest."

(Children stand in semi-circle U C. Very young children may have an older child in center as their leader.)

I   Hold arms as if cradling a baby. Double balance forward and back. (Double balance is: step forward R. Bring L up to R. Rise on toes; sink down on heels. Step back L. Bring R up to L. Rise on toes, down on heels.) Turn in individual circle in place to R, with tiny steps on toes, holding arms slightly higher to R. `- - - - - - - -` (1-4)   4 meas.
Double balance, starting L and turn to L. `- - - - - -` (5-8)   4 meas.

II Double balance forward and back.
   Walk forward - - - - - - - - - - - - - - (9-12) 4 meas.
   Double balance forward and back.
   Walk back - - - - - - - - - - - - - - (13-16) 4 meas.

                        16 meas.

III Double balance forward and back. Turn to R as in I.
   Double balance forward and back. Turn to L as in I. (1-8) 8 meas.

IV Single balance to R on R, lifting L off floor and holding baby up to R.
   Balance back on L, holding baby up L. - - - - - - (9-10) 2 meas.
   Step to R on R, swing L forward to R side.
   Lunge forward on L.
   Kneel on R knee—L knee up, rocking arms from side to side.
   Kneel on both knees—Sit back on heels.
   Make gestures of placing baby in crib, drawing up cover and of
   a Good-night prayer. ("Lay thee down now and rest, May thy
   slumber be blest.") - - - - - - - - - - - - - (11-16) 6 meas.

                        16 meas.

Lullaby

JOH. BRAHMS

TWO LITTLE COLONELS

"Two Little Colonels"

(A dance for two or more children, age 5-7, based on the movie, featuring Shirley Temple in "The Little Colonel". Costume, 1860 Period, ruffled pantalettes, full or hoop skirt, poke bonnet and lace mits. This dance has a great appeal to the children because of their interest in the movie.)

Minuet—Op. Posth. 12, No. 1 by Schubert.

I   Both stand side by side U C and face forward.
  (a) Slide-close-step-point—(Point R foot to side, bending body to R—R hand
      L - R - L - R   down—L hand up)
  (Child on L side)
  Both dance away from partner. Child on R dances same movement to R.
  (b) Repeat slide-close-step-point (toward partner)
      R - L - R - L
  (c) Three slides to L and point R to R side.
    (Each little girl does this same movement to R and L sides respec-
    tively. Second child does 3 slides R and pt. L). - - - - (1-4)   4 meas.
    Repeat a, b, and c, dancing toward partner, away from partner and
    meeting in center. At end of phrase, both curtsey - - - (5-8)   4 meas.

                                                  8 meas.

II   Both face forward and join inside hands.
  (a) Slide-close-step, lifting foot off floor in back
      R - L - R - L
  Slide-close-step, lifting foot in front, knee bent.
      L - R - L - R
  Run forward and balance in arabesque. - - - - - (1-4)   4 meas.
  (b) Repeat same movement.
  Slide-close-step, balancing backward, forward and then running backward.
  Curtsey to audience at end of phrase. - - - - - - (5-8)   4 meas.

                                         Repeat 8 meas.

III   Face partner—Join R hands
  (a) Double balance forward and back
    (Double balance is—Step forward R—Bring L up to R—Rise on toes—Down on heels.
    Step back on L—Bring R up to L—Rise on toes—Down on heels)
    One child makes complete turn U S under lifted arm of other child.
    Both curtsey to partner. - - - - - - - - - (9-12)   4 meas.

(b) Join L hands
   Double balance forward and back.   Second child repeats turn
   toward audience. Both curtsey. · · · · · · · · ·   (13-16)   4 meas.

                                                                          8 meas.

IV   Both face forward, hands on hats

   (a) Double balance forward and back
       Turn in separate small circles, with tiny steps in place, holding
       skirt and curtsey. · · · · · · · · · · · · ·   (9-12)   4 meas.

   (b) Join inside hands
       Double balance forward and back
       Run forward and curtsey · · · · · · · · · ·   (13-16)   4 meas.

                                                             Repeat   8 meas.

Music Dixie—1 Verse and 2 choruses
       Both finish D C.

   (a) Separate—1 polka to R and 1 to L in semi-circle, finishing U C
       (Polka here used is—Hop-slide-close
       Hop L with lifted R knee—slide R and close L.
       Hop R with lifted L knee—slide L and close R.) · · · · · ·   1 verse

   (b) Meet U C.   Join both hands
       Polka in small circle. · · · · · · · · · · · · ·   1 chorus

   (c) Both face forward—Raise R hands as if waving a flag
       Polka in place—(Raise R knee—step R-L-R (12 meas.)
                       Raise L knee simultaneously with step on R
                       Repeat starting L)
       Polka forward as in (a) and salute (4 meas.) · · · · · ·   1 chorus

Two Little Colonels
Minuet

FR. SCHUBERT

Photography by Arnett

PLAYING STATUE
Figure I

Statues

Statues, statues, all in a row,
　　Statues, statues, standing so.
Tell me, tell me, are you wise,
　　Have all these statues seeing eyes?

Every day when school is done,
　　Playing "Statues" is such fun.
We skip and run and balance so
　　And then we pose all in a row.

Statues, statues, strong and straight,
　　Statues, I have counted eight.
Tell me, tell me, will we grow
　　Like these statues posing so?

Will we come to life and be
　　Lovely statues all can see?
Will we be so fine and high
　　That our statues touch the sky?

L. L.

Photography by Arnett

Figure II

Figure III

Playing Statue

Dance for seven

Music—Schubert
Ecossaisen Op. 18 a
No. 1, 2, 3.
Op. 67, No. 1

Introduction.   Seven children are standing in groups of 2, 3, 2, as though playing.   They may be holding hands or have their arms around each others waists.

Floor Pattern

```
           172
53         000        46
00                    00
```

Ecossaisen
Op. 18 a, No. 1

I   Leader No. 7 and first child join right hands and skip around.   At end of
phrase, child falls into pose of statue.   meas. 1-8 ⁄ ⁄ ⁄ ⁄ ⁄ ⁄ ⁄ ⁄   8 meas.
Leader turns second child with a skip.   meas. 1-8 *Repeated* ⁄ ⁄ ⁄ ⁄ ⁄   8 meas.
Leader turns third child with a skip.   meas. 9-16 ⁄ ⁄ ⁄ ⁄ ⁄ ⁄ ⁄   8 meas.
Leader turns fourth child with a skip.   meas. 9-16 *Repeated* ⁄ ⁄ ⁄ ⁄ ⁄   8 meas.
Leader turns fifth child with a skip.   meas. 1-8 ⁄ ⁄ ⁄ ⁄ ⁄ ⁄ ⁄   8 meas.
Leader turns sixth child with a skip.   meas. 9-16 ⁄ ⁄ ⁄ ⁄ ⁄ ⁄ ⁄   8 meas.

At end of phrase children take position of some well known statue.
(For dance quality, children may skip like Harriet Frishmuth's "The Dancers", holding R hand tightly, leaning back, and with L hands beckoning partner to dance on and on.   See page 91.)   Turn according to numbers as 5 and 6 are more difficult for young children to hold.
Formation at end of first figure.   (See illustration page 119.)

```
5       12       6
0       00       0
    30       04
```

1 and 2 (Two central figures) "Flower Holder" by Karl Gruppe
3 and 4 (Seated D S to R and L of Central figures)—"Evening"—
                                        *Painting by Maxfield Parrish
5 and 6 (Figures to R and L of center) "Joy of the Waters"—By Harriet Frishmuth.

*Note: These paintings should be shown to the children and taught as paintings.   It would be wise to substitute a triangular seated figure, such as the sculpture, "Repose", by Jennewein, or "Reverie", by Grace Talbot.

[127]

Children hold positions while leader looks at statues to decide which she likes best.

Skip-hold.   (Leader stops at statue No. 4 and shakes head, as if it doesn't please her) ⁻ ⁻ ⁻ ⁻ ⁻ ⁻ ⁻ ⁻ ⁻ ⁻ (meas. 1)

Skip-hold.   Repeat with statue No. 3 ⁻ ⁻ ⁻ ⁻ ⁻ (meas. 2)

Step-step-hold, in skipping position.   Leader looks at statue 5 and shakes head in disapproval ⁻ ⁻ ⁻ ⁻ ⁻ ⁻ ⁻ ⁻ (meas. 3-4)

A continuous skip.   Leader skips in and out, stopping at statue 6

(meas. 5-8)   8 meas.

Leader skips around again and falls into pose of chosen statue, C C.   Statue, seated on floor, should be chosen each time in order to balance the picture ⁻ ⁻ ⁻ ⁻ ⁻ ⁻ ⁻ ⁻ ⁻ (meas. 9-16)   8 meas.

Floor Pattern

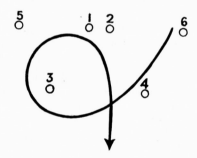

Statues all come to life and run over to leader ⁻ ⁻ (meas. 9-10)

One child takes her hand and lifts her up ⁻ ⁻ ⁻ (meas. 11-12)

Children run quickly back to places ⁻ ⁻ ⁻ ⁻ (meas. 13-16)   8 meas.
repeated

The chosen statue becomes the new leader.   The first leader takes her place in the figure.

Play Ecossaisen No. 2 for Second Figure
Repeat No. 3 Interlude

II   New leader skips children into second formation.   At end of figure, leader skips around and chooses statue.   The chosen statue becomes leader for third figure.

Formation at end of second figure.   (See illustration page 123.   See sculpture photographs pages 91 and 89.)

1 and 2 (Two central figures)—"The Dancers" by Harriet Frishmuth

5 and 6 (Figures standing to R and L of center)—"Crest of the Wave" by Harriet Frishmuth

3 and 4 (Seated D S to L and R of center)—"Morning," painting by Maxfield Parrish

III Third Formation. (See illustration page 125. See sculpture photographs pages 63 and 85.)

1 and 2—"Flower Holder" by Maude Jewett

3 and 4—"Memory" by Dillons

5 and 6—"Aspiration" by Bonnie MacLeary

At end of this Figure leader runs off stage U L and statues hold positions.

Music for Interlude. Op. 18 a No. 3

Music for Second Figure   *Ecossaisen Op. 18 a No. 2*

Leader turns first child with a skip. meas. 1-8   ✓ ✓ ✓ ✓ ✓ ✓ ✓ ✓   8 meas.

Leader turns second child with a skip. meas. 1-8   ✓ ✓ ✓ ✓ ✓ ✓ ✓ ✓   8 meas.

Leader turns third child with a skip. meas. 9-16   ✓ ✓ ✓ ✓ ✓ ✓ ✓ ✓   8 meas.

Leader turns fourth child with a skip. meas. 9-16   ✓ ✓ ✓ ✓ ✓ ✓ ✓ ✓   8 meas.

Leader turns fifth child with a skip. meas. 1-8   ✓ ✓ ✓ ✓ ✓ ✓ ✓ ✓   8 meas.

Leader turns sixth child with a skip. meas. 9-16   ✓ ✓ ✓ ✓ ✓ ✓ ✓ ✓   8 meas.

Interlude—   *Repeat Ecossaisen Op. 18 a, No. 3*

New leader chooses statue.

Music for Third Figure   *Ecossaisen Op. 67 No. 1*

Leader turns first child with a skip. meas. 1-8   ✓ ✓ ✓ ✓ ✓ ✓ ✓ ✓   8 meas.

Leader turns second child with a skip. meas. 1-8   ✓ ✓ ✓ ✓ ✓ ✓ ✓ ✓   8 meas.

Leader turns third child with a skip. meas. 9-16   ✓ ✓ ✓ ✓ ✓ ✓ ✓ ✓   8 meas.

Leader turns fourth child with a skip. meas. 9-16   ✓ ✓ ✓ ✓ ✓ ✓ ✓ ✓   8 meas.

Leader turns fifth child with a skip. meas. 1-8   ✓ ✓ ✓ ✓ ✓ ✓ ✓ ✓   8 meas.

Leader turns sixth child with a skip. meas. 9-18   ✓ ✓ ✓ ✓ ✓ ✓ ✓ ✓   8 meas.

Playing Statue
Fig. I

"Ecossaisen"
FR. SCHUBERT
Op. 18ª, Nº1

Nº3. Interlude

Playing Statue
Fig. II

"Ecossaisen"
FR. SCHUBERT
Op. 18ª, Nº 2

Figure III

Op. 67, Nº 1

To a Gossip

If you knew that the words you said
Ranged themselves about my bed
Like terrible shadows, cold and grey,
I feel sure that the words you say
Would always be lovely, happy and gay.

Truth rings out in the sound of your voice,
Your eyes can make my heart rejoice,
Your hands have made me glad to-day,
But over and over again, I say,
Do you know how much a word can weigh?

L. L.

Photography by Arnett

GOSSIP

Gossip

Dance for four
A dramatic dance

Music—*"Dance of the Reed Pipes"
from "The Nut Cracker
Suite" by Tschaikowsky.*

(A dramatic dance with much pantomime. Movements are staccato and are executed with precision, like marionettes. Four dancers, two couples, costumed in old fashioned dress like that of the sixties, stiff little hats made of sateen-covered buckram, edged with lace, tip-tilted on head and tied under chin with ribbon. Each dancer wears a little fan, on a ribbon around her neck.)

Floor Plan

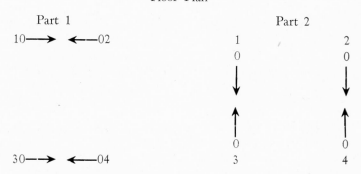

Part 1

Part 2

Dancers stand in place in square formation.

Introduction—Look around to see who is there   · · · · · · ·   meas. 1 and 2

I Bow, effusive nods and smiles to rhythm of music · · · · · ·   meas. 3

Fan in rhythm · · · · · · · · · · · · ·   meas. 4

Walk, stiff-kneed, swinging opposite arm, toward partner and meeting in center · · · · · · · · · · · · · ·   meas. 5

1 and 2 walk toward each other as shown in diagram.

3 and 4 walk toward each other as shown in diagram.

Shake hands very stiffly · · · · · · · · · · · ·   meas. 6

(Dancer No. 1 makes gesture of telling something to No. 2) · ·   meas. 7

(No. 3 whispers to No. 4) · · · · · · · · · ·   meas. 7

See picture page 96.

(Both stand on tip-toe, feet together, lean forward. No. 1 has R hand curved at mouth, L hand extended back, slightly below shoulder level.)

(No. 2 has R hand at ear, L hand extended back. This makes opposition movement. 1 faces audience. 2 has back to audience.)

(No. 2 whispers to No. 1)   ‑ ‑ ‑ ‑ ‑ ‑ ‑ ‑ ‑ ‑ ‑ ‑ ‑   meas. 8
(No. 4 whispers to No. 3)   ‑ ‑ ‑ ‑ ‑ ‑ ‑ ‑ ‑ ‑ ‑ ‑   meas. 8
All four dancers raise both hands in front of chest, elbows bent,
palms turned out in gesture of surprise. Lowering arms, run back
to place and turn to face new partner ‑ ‑ ‑ ‑ ‑ ‑ ‑ ‑   meas. 9‑10

10 meas.

II   Repeat the same complete figure with new partner ‑ ‑ ‑ ‑   meas. 11‑18
     1 and 3 are partners
     2 and 4 are partners   8 meas.

III   1 and 2 are again partners
     3 and 4 are again partners
     Instead of bowing, put hands curved at mouth, meaning, "I have
     something to tell you" ‑ ‑ ‑ ‑ ‑ ‑ ‑ ‑ ‑ ‑ ‑ ‑   meas. 19
     Instead of fanning, put one hand at ear, other extended back,
     meaning, "Will you listen?" ‑ ‑ ‑ ‑ ‑ ‑ ‑ ‑ ‑ ‑ ‑   meas. 20
     Walk to center and meet partner ‑ ‑ ‑ ‑ ‑ ‑ ‑ ‑ ‑   meas. 21
     Instead of shaking hands again, stand on tip‑toe, hands at each side,
     palms parallel with floor, fingers together and pointing out, heads
     close together and lips nearly touching, as though each is eager to
     tell a new bit of gossip. Hold in this position ‑ ‑ ‑ ‑ ‑   meas. 22
     (1 whispers to 2) ‑ ‑ ‑ ‑ ‑ ‑ ‑ ‑ ‑ ‑ ‑ ‑ ‑   meas. 23
     (3 whispers to 4) ‑ ‑ ‑ ‑ ‑ ‑ ‑ ‑ ‑ ‑ ‑ ‑ ‑   meas. 23
     (2 whispers to 1) ‑ ‑ ‑ ‑ ‑ ‑ ‑ ‑ ‑ ‑ ‑ ‑ ‑   meas. 24
     (4 whispers to 3) ‑ ‑ ‑ ‑ ‑ ‑ ‑ ‑ ‑ ‑ ‑ ‑ ‑   meas. 24
     Walk back to place, hands lifted as in 1 ‑ ‑ ‑ ‑ ‑ ‑ ‑   meas. 25‑26

(19‑26)   8 meas.

     Look around to see who is there—Whirl around in place and
     end facing new partner ‑ ‑ ‑ ‑ ‑ ‑ ‑ ‑ ‑ ‑ ‑ ‑   meas. 27‑29

3 meas.

IV   1 and 3 are partners
     2 and 4 are partners
     Both have hands curved at mouth, "I have something to tell you"   meas. 30
     Both look around to see who is coming ‑ ‑ ‑ ‑ ‑ ‑ ‑   meas. 31
     Walk to meet partner ‑ ‑ ‑ ‑ ‑ ‑ ‑ ‑ ‑ ‑ ‑ ‑   meas. 32
     (omit hold)
     1 whispers to 3 ‑ ‑ ‑ ‑ ‑ ‑ ‑ ‑ ‑ ‑ ‑ ‑ ‑   meas. 33
     2 whispers to 4 ‑ ‑ ‑ ‑ ‑ ‑ ‑ ‑ ‑ ‑ ‑ ‑ ‑   meas. 33
     3 whispers to 1 (same position as 1) ‑ ‑ ‑ ‑ ‑ ‑ ‑   meas. 34
     4 whispers to 2 ‑ ‑ ‑ ‑ ‑ ‑ ‑ ‑ ‑ ‑ ‑ ‑ ‑   meas. 34
     Run back to place as in 1 ‑ ‑ ‑ ‑ ‑ ‑ ‑ ‑ ‑ ‑ ‑   meas. 35

(30‑35)   6 meas.

Ending—1, 3 and 4 run to center and stand in circle formation, on tip-toe, hands at sides, fingers pointing out, heads close together, all whispering · · · · · · · · · · · · · meas. 36

2 walks off U L as though she doesn't approve of gossip · · · meas. 37

_____

2 meas.

Gossip

"Dance of the Reed Pipes"*
from the "Nutcracker Suite"
TSCHAIKOWSKY

* Transcribed for piano by Franz C. Bornschein

Photography by Arnett

MAZURKA

Mazurka

Dance composition

Music—*La Czarine*
by *Louis Ganne*

For six or eight

(A very gay, spirited dance with marked rhythm and varied movement.)

Costume

Girl—Short full skirt, made of golden yellow silk, coming above knee and trimmed with three bands of red ribbon at bottom; tight fitting yellow knickers, white longsleeved blouse, trimmed in red braid; red sateen bodice, laced up with black velvet ribbon; boots, made of red oil cloth; black slippers with heels; yellow silk triangular scarf headdress.

Boy—Red sateen "shorts", red oil cloth boots, black slippers, white longsleeved blouse, red sateen bolero, bound with gold braid, sash and triangular scarf headdress, made of striped material in harmonizing shades.

Dance Description

Mazurka Step danced to R; opposite to L
Step R to R side—count 1
Slide L up to R—count 2
Jump L, clicking heels—count 3   (1 meas.)
Twostep turn and stamp (to R) (Opposite to L)
Step R, step L, stamp R
Change arm position while turning. Bring R hand above head, L hand on hip.
Formation—3 dancers R side; three dancers L side
Dancers change sides with 3 Mazurka steps, two step turn and stamp.

Introduction. Hands on hips. 3 stamps in place. Accent count 1

    Repeat   ́ ́ ́ ́ ́ ́ ́ ́ ́ ́ ́ ́ ́   (2 meas.)
I   Three Mazurka steps, twostep turn and stamp   ́ ́ ́ (14)   4 meas.
     Repeat three times, changing sides each time ́ ́ ́ (516)   12 meas.
     (Dancing to R—R hand on hip—L hand high above head. —————
       Dancing to L—L hand on hip—R hand high above head.)   16 meas.

II   Same formation—3 each side
All whirl toward center. Face partner, R arms around waists,
L arms high. Stamp 3 ‚ ‚ ‚ ‚ ‚ ‚ ‚ ‚ ‚ ‚ ‚ ‚ ‚ ‚ ‚   4 meas.
Whirl around, same position, with a slight dipping motion to
rhythm of music. Stamp 3 ‚ ‚ ‚ ‚ ‚ ‚ ‚ ‚ ‚ ‚ ‚ ‚   4 meas.
Whirl back to places—stamp 3, hands on hips ‚ ‚ ‚ ‚ ‚ ‚   4 meas.
Whirl in place and stamp 3 ‚ ‚ ‚ ‚ ‚ ‚ ‚ ‚ ‚ ‚ ‚ ‚ ‚   4 meas.

                                                             (17-32)   16 meas.

(Note—When couples whirl to center, U S couple No. 3 dances
in center. Middle couple No. 2 dances slightly to L; D S couple
No. 1 dances slightly to R)

III   Repeat step 1 four times
(3 Mazurka steps—Two-step turn and stamp)
Finish step meeting partner
Couple 3 U S couple center
Couple 2 Middle couple on L
Couple 1 D S couple on R ‚ ‚ ‚ ‚ ‚ ‚ ‚ ‚ ‚ ‚   (33-48)   16 meas

IV   Couple 3 U S couple dance first to L, then R, then L and R.
Couples No. 1 and 2 change places.
Couple No. 1 dances across stage to L
Couple No. 2 dances across stage to R
Girl stands in front of boy. Both face forward and extend arms
shoulder level. Boy holds girl's hands.
Step danced to L (Opposite to R)
Step L to L side—Draw R up to L
Repeat twice. Let go R hands, girl makes a complete turn under
boys L arm ‚   4 meas.
Repeat above step three times.
On the last turn, the boy places his R hand on the girl's R hip and
both make a four-step turn to R ‚ ‚ ‚ ‚ ‚ ‚ ‚ ‚ ‚ ‚ ‚ ‚   12 meas.

                                                             (49-64)   16 meas.

V   This step is danced in circular formation with partner.
Girl stands on boy's R. Arms around waists. Both step forward
L, raise R knee, lunge forward R, raise L knee.
Boy stands in place. Girl does 3 step turn (step L R L) to boy's
L side. Both stamp in place 3 (R L R) ‚ ‚ ‚ ‚ ‚ ‚ ‚ ‚   4 meas.
Repeat this step 3 times ‚ ‚ ‚ ‚ ‚ ‚ ‚ ‚ (Omit repeat) 12 meas.

                                                             (65-80)   16 meas.

Interlude—Go into formation ‚ ‚ ‚ ‚ ‚ ‚ ‚ ‚   (81-84)   4 meas.

(For eight dancers—wheel formation
Boys kneel, facing out in circle; girls weave in and out.)

For six dancers
1 boy kneels center, facing forward.
Two boys kneel Right and Left sides, respectively. Both face center.
Girls stand in line formation to L.
Boys extend R arms, as if proposing to girls.
Girls weave in and out, finally accepting original partner.

VI Girls dance this step (Desc. to R, opposite to L)
Step R to R side—Draw L up to R—Step R to R side, making
½ turn R.
Step L to L side—Draw R up to L—Step L to L side, completing
turn to R.
Whirl around, making a turn and a half to R. - - - - - - - - 4 meas.
Repeat 3 times - - - - - - - - - - - - - - - - - 12 meas.

                                            (85-100)   16 meas.

Girls join R hands with boys. Boys rise. Face partner. Boys
have their hands clasped around girls' waists, girls' hands on boys'
shoulders.
Boys and girls dance together, same step. Repeat music (85-100) 16 meas.

VII Play first theme again.
Formation—six dancers on R.
(Desc. to L, opposite to R)
Step L, draw R up to L—hop R, at same time, raise L leg to side,
knee bent and extend.
Repeat twice.
Hands on hips, stamp 3.
All dance this step to L - - - - - - - - - - - - - - 4 meas.
Repeat to R; repeat to L - - - - - - - - - - - - - 8 meas.
Three dancers whirl in place L
Other three dance Mazurka step to R
All stamp 3 - - - - - - - - - - - - - - - - - 4 meas.

                                            (101-116) 16 meas.

Dancers on R, raise R arm, L hand on hip, as they stamp.
Dancers on L, raise L arm, R hand on hip.

Mazurka
La Czarine

Introduction
ben marcato

LOUIS GANNE

[149]

When I Dance Statues

"I know the gleam of chiseled marble,
I feel the strength of polished bronze,
I live the eternity of crystaled movement,
Secured with beauty's fragile bonds.

I suffer remorse with perverse Salome,
I lead in the hunt by Diana's leave,
I rise with the languor of Unconquered Venice,
And weep with the tears of rebellious Eve.

I skip on the foam of a crashing wave,
I kneel in the curve of a fluted bowl,
I reach for the gleam of a beckoning star,
Like Icarus seek the flaming goal.

I freeze a melting dancing rhythm,
I sculpt a gallery's proud array,
I fashion statues of infinite beauty,
And mould them in finite human clay."

AT THE MUSEUM
Series I—Figure I

At the Museum

A dance of sculpture

Music—Schubert Waltzes
Part 1—Deutsche Tänze Op. 33, No. 2
Part 2—Op. 9b, No. 11
Part 3—Valses Sentimentales Op. 50, No. 4
Part 4—Same as 1

The idea of this number appeals to the children's imagination. The statue dance teaches balance, precision, of movement, smoothness and design in detail, such as careful movements of hands, feet, arms, etc.

Costume—The children wear blue silk tunics. The statues wear flesh colored leotards. The frieze is most effective against a black back drop.

Motivation—When the curtain opens, five children (the statues) in leotards, form a beautiful frieze of sculpture U C. They hold their positions during parts 1 and 2.

Part I Six children (or any number desired) walk into the museum. They enter walking naturally in groups of 1, 2, and 3. They look at the statues, admire their beauty and decide to dance to show their appreciation. Music No. 1 - - - - - - - - - (meas. 1-16) 16 meas.

Part II The Children's Dance (Music No. 2)

1 Children dance across stage from L to R.
Hop R, at same time, raising L leg off floor and swinging arms up R in arabesque position.
Step L, step R, hop R, swinging L leg forward and both arms to L side.
Whirl around R, bringing R arm in circular movement to R - 4 meas.
Repeat, starting L - - - - - - - - - - - - - - 4 meas.

(meas. 1-8) 8 meas.

2 Children dance across stage from R to L
Hop R, L knee bent and arms high above head
Hop L, R knee bent and arms at sides, fingers together and pointing out.
Whirl around to R, keeping arms and hands at side - - - - 4 meas.
Repeat L - - - - - - - - - - - - - - - - - 4 meas.

(meas. 9-16) 8 meas.

3 (a) Children dance in circle
Hop R, swing L up and back in arabesque position, arms held
high and forward

(b) Hop L, swing R forward, knee extended, arms back; bend over
slightly.
Whirl around R, circling arms and unfolding - - - - - - 4 meas.
Repeat (b) then (a) - - - - - - - - - - - - - 4 meas.

(meas. 17-24) 8 meas.

Repeat 2 and 3 circle - - - - - - - - - (meas. 9-24) 16 meas.
The children grow tired waiting for their mothers to come and fall asleep.
They may take any reclining position of decorative value. The ones
we used were based on the paintings: "A Naiad" by Henner, "Bacchante
by the Sea" by Corot and others by Maxfield Parrish. Music—same as
part 1.

Part III   The Sculpture Dance—Music No. 3.
While the children are asleep, they dream that the statues come to life
and dance for them. The positions of the statues are based on 28 famous
sculptures. The movements are legato; the frieze decorative, with one
central figure and two figures on each side. The side figures repeat the
same motif on each side. Each statue does a series of four movements
to eight measures of music.

Five children
O O O O O
a b c b a

All face center
Series repeated on each side
Series I meas. 1-8
Statues a
1 Jeanne d'Arc—Chapu
2 Reverie—Grace Talbot
3 Narcissus—Emory Seidel
4 Salome—Grace Talbot
Statues b
1 Memory—Dillons
2 The Dragon Fly—Rachel M. Hawks
3 Fragilina—Attilio Piccirilli
4 Atalanta—Mario Korbel
Statues c
1 Descending Night—Adolph Weinman
2 Evening—Ruckstall
3 Study in Rose Marble—Bilotti
4 Reflections—Harriet W. Frishmuth

Series II meas. 9-16

Statues a
1 Allegra—Frishmuth
2 Scherzo—Frishmuth
3 Crest of the Wave—Frishmuth—page 89
4 Joy of the Waters—Frishmuth

Statues b
1 Arabesque—Harriet W. Frishmuth
2 Laughing Waters—Frishmuth
3 Dancing Woman—Prahar
4 Butterfly—Emil Fuchs

Statues c
1 The Golden Hour—Evans
2 Unfettered—Albin Polasek
3 Aspiration—Bonnie MacLeary—page 63
4 Extase—Frishmuth

Series III Statues come out of frieze
Two side figures hold position of "Play Days" by Harriet Frishmuth
Three central figures dance "Allegresse" by Bessie Potter Vonnoh—
page 77
Figure on L turns under central figure's arm
Figure on R turns under central figure's arm
Central figure whirls around
Repeat above figure
All whirl around and go into next formation (meas. 17-24)　　-　8 meas.

Series IV
Central figure holds position of "The Star" by Frishmuth
Four figures (2 each side) dance "Andante" by Korbel—page 65
Hold position of "Andante" 2 meas.
Turn one measure
Hold one measure
Turn one measure
Hold one measure
Turn and go into original frieze 2 meas. (meas. 17-24)　-　-　-　8 meas.

Part IV

The statues are quite still in their frieze. The children wake up and
look all around, as if to say, "Did you see what I saw?" They come up
slowly to sitting positions, rise, look lovingly at the statues and walk
reluctantly out of the museum.

Music same as I

[159]

At the Museum

FR. SCHUBERT
Op. 33, № 2

Op. 9, № 11

* Play I, II, I, III, I.

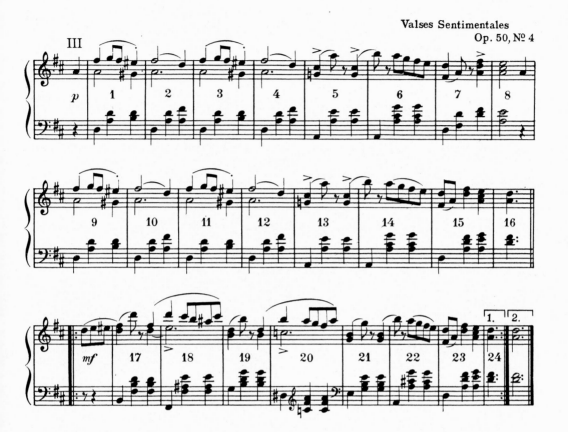

References for Sculpture in "At the Museum"

Apollo—An Illustrated Manual of the History of Art Throughout the Ages by
Reinach—Scribners
JEANNE D'ARC by Chapu—page 326

Atalanta by Joseph Mario Korbel
Photograph from deWitt Ward, 227 W. 13th St., N. Y. C.
Joseph Mario Korbel, 54 West 74th St., N. Y. C.

Books on Sculpture by Lorado Taft, Library

Contemporary American Sculpture—Copyright 1929 by "The National Sculp-
ture Society"—Kalkhoff Press, N. Y.
ANDANTE by Joseph Mario Korbel—page 188
FRAGILINA by Attilio Piccirilli—page 255
PLAY DAYS by Harriet W. Frishmuth—page 123
STUDY IN ROSE MARBLE by S. F. Bilotti—page 27
UNFETTERED by Albin Polasek—page 261

Detroit Institute of Arts—Detroit, Michigan
L'ALLEGRESSE by Bessie Potter Vonnoh—see photograph page 77

Famous Small Bronzes—A beautiful book, containing forty-eight sculpture photo-
graphs, may be purchased from The Gorham Company, Fifth Avenue and
47th St., for one dollar.
BUTTERFLY by Emil Fuchs—page 69
CREST OF THE WAVE by Harriet W. Frishmuth—page 13
JOY OF THE WATERS by Harriet W. Frishmuth—page 103
PLAY DAYS by Harriet W. Frishmuth—page 43
THE STAR by Harriet W. Frishmuth—page 35

Grand Central Galleries—Fifth Avenue and 51st St., N. Y. C., or 15 Vanderbilt
Ave., N. Y. C—Photographs of sculpture:—
REVERIE by Grace Helen Talbot
SALOME by Grace Helen Talbot

Memory by Dillons—See photograph, illustrating dance.

Metropolitan Museum of Art—Fifth Avenue, N. Y. C.
Photographs, ten cents each:—
ANDANTE by Mario Korbel
ASPIRATION by Bonnie MacLeary
DANCING WOMAN by Prahar
EVENING by Ruckstall
FRAGILINA by Attilio Piccirilli
THE GOLDEN HOUR by Evans

Small Bronzes by Great Sculptors as Prizes—Grand Central Galleries—15
Vanderbilt Avenue, N. Y. C. A booklet, price twenty-five cents.
DESCENDING NIGHT by Adolph Weinman
THE STAR by Harriet W. Frishmuth

"Tait McKenzie—A Sculptor of Youth"—A book of athletic figures, price,
$3.75, formerly ten dollars. This book may also be purchased from John
Archinal, book seller, 2014 Pine Street, Philadelphia, Pa. The Gorham
Company usually keeps a small supply on hand.

The Dragon Fly by Rachel M. Hawks
EDUCATIONAL DANCE SERIES by Lucile and Agnes Marsh, published by
J. Fischer and Bro., N. Y. C., or The Gorham Company

The Gorham Company, Bronze Division, 6 West 48th St., N. Y. C.
Photographs, five cents each:—
ALLEGRA by Harriet W. Frishmuth
ARABESQUE by Harriet W. Frishmuth
EXTASE by Harriet W. Frishmuth
LAUGHING WATERS by Harriet W. Frishmuth
REFLECTIONS by Harriet W. Frishmuth
SCHERZO by Harriet W. Frishmuth
NARCISSUS by Emory Seidel

A Cup of Joy

Life lets down her silver cup of joy
Behold! I stand on tip-toe,
Drinking from its shining brim.
Speak! Are you asleep?
Wake up and look for joy.
Life will give you far more joy
Than you can dream.
Look! Can't you see
Joy spilling everywhere!
Stretch out your hands for joy.

L. L.

Photography by Arnett

A Cup of Joy

"A Cup of Joy"

Dance-Poem

Dance Movement—Movements are done as reader, who is off stage, reads lines. Group of three dancers, U C.

Property—A silver bowl, shaped like a large cup. A china bowl, painted inside and out with silver paint, may be used.

Costume—Life, who is much taller than the other two figures, wears a long blue robe and silver Grecian sandals. She may have a wreath of flowers in her hair. The other two figures wear short tunics of light blue made Grecian style. They are barefooted. The robe is of heavy satin, a deeper shade than the other two figures' draperies, which are of china silk.

There is no musical accompaniment.

Figure when curtain rises:—

Life stands in center, facing front, cup held high above head, wrists touching, fingers together.

The child designated as Figure I represents the Spirit of Joy. She is seated to R of Life. She takes the position of "Morning", a painting by Maxfield Parrish. See picture, page 167. Child is seated on floor, feet together, knees bent, hands clasped around knees, head up. Figure II represents the spirit of Gloom or Depression. She is seated to L of Life. She takes the position of "Reverie", sculpture by Grace Talbot. Sit back on heels, head down and turned slightly to R, hands clasped in back.

Line I.—*Life lets down her silver cup of joy.*

Life lowers cup about two inches above head, by bending elbows.

Line II—*Behold! I stand on tip-toe, drinking from its shining brim.*

Life turns to her R and lowers cup for child to drink. Keep arms in circular position, U S arm higher. Hold cup in tilted position. Figure I rises by extending R leg. Push forward on L knee. Place L knee on floor and rise to both feet. Stand on tip-toe, lips close to cup, hands at each side, palms down and parallel with floor, fingers together, pointing out, wrists touching body, like "Wild Flower", sculpture by Edward Berge. Figure II keeps same position.

Line III—*Speak! Are you asleep?*

Life continues turn to her R and holds cup high above head back to audience. Figure II, same position.

Figure I walks over to II and kneels (between Life and II). Both knees bent, L knee on floor, R knee up, toes bent, R foot slightly below L knee. Figure I extends L arm and takes L hand of II, R arm extended to R side.

Line IV—*Wake up and look for joy.*
> Life has same position as in Line III.
> I lifts II up. Figure II rises to both knees, then raises L foot and comes all the way up.

Line V—*Life will give you far more joy than you can dream.*
> Life finishes turn to R and faces front. She then turns toward Figure II, and holds cup in position of pouring joy in child's hands. Continues to keep arms in circular position, representing eternity. Figure II stands with D S (L) knee bent, elbows bent and touching body, hands together, fingers cupped to hold joy. Figure I walks backward to place.

Line VI—*Look! Can't you see? Joy spilling everywhere!*
> Life circles cup front, to R side and holds it high above head, tilted so that audience can see bottom of cup. Figure I takes two steps back, turns to her L (opposite from the way the cup is swung). She pauses, back to audience, both arms stretched out to side, as though looking at a light. Finish turn to L. End facing front.
> Figure II walks back two steps and stands, arms down and slightly back. She is looking up at Life.

Line VII—*Stretch out your hands for joy!*
> Life, same position as in Line VI.
> Both children run forward with outstretched hands.

Photography by Arnett

PLAY

A STUDY IN DESIGN

Play

A dance of play for three or six dancers

Music—Schubert Waltz, Op. 9b, No. 15

Introduction—Three dancers are standing in a line U C, holding joined hands high above heads.

I   Leap-step-together forward · · · · · · · · · · · · · · meas. 1
       1 small leap forward on R foot · · · · · · · · count 1
       1 step forward on L foot · · · · · · · · · · count 2
       Bring R up to L · · · · · · · · · · · · count 3

       Leap-step-together backward · · · · · · · · · · · meas. 2
       1 small leap back on L foot · · · · · · · · · · count 1
       1 step back on R foot · · · · · · · · · · count 2
       Bring L up to R · · · · · · · · · · · · count 3

       Dancers 1 2 3
              o o o
       Dancers 2 and 3 continue to leap-step-together forward and back.
       At same time, dancer No. 1 runs D C under arch, made by joined
       hands of 2 and 3 · · · · · · · · · · · · · · · meas. 3-4

---

                                                           4 meas.

       All 3 dancers continue to leap-step-together, forward and back.
       2 and 3 U C—1 D C · · · · · · · · · · · · · meas. 5-6
       No. 1 looks first over R shoulder, then over L, as though to say,
       "You can't catch me."

       2 and 3 run forward · · · · · · · · · · · · · meas. 7
       While 2 and 3 are running forward, dancer 1 does leap-step-together
       once and holds in place D C.

       2 and 3 catch 1 and take position of "Flower Holder," sculpture by
       Maude Jewett. No. 1 is in center of "Flower Holder," arms
       curved in circle above head, hands, palms down, one hand under the
       other. See picture, page 171, central figures · · · · · · meas. 8

---

                                                           4 meas.

II   Position for figure · · · · · 2 1 3

1 is in center.
2 is on 1's R.
3 is on 1's L.

Dancers 2 and 3 open D S arms, joining hands with 1.
1 and 2 join R hands.
1 and 3 join L hands.
3 joins her R hand with 2's L.

This makes dancer No. 1 the leader.
The next figure is like "Follow the Leader" and is danced in a circle
around the stage.
No. 1 is in position of pulling dancers 2 and 3 forward.
See picture, page 173, end figures.

All leap-step-together forward twice · · · · · · · · · meas. 9-10
Then 2 and 3 lift arms, L and R hands joined respectively, and let
1 go back and under.
2 and 3 make a complete turn under their own arms.
2 turns under her L arm, 3 turns under her R arm.
These turns are made very quickly.
Continue to hold hands as in first figure.
This makes 2 and 3 the leaders · · · · · · · · · meas. 11-12

                                                            4 meas.

Continue to leap-step-together forward twice · · · · · · meas. 13-14
Turn under · · · · · · · · · · · · · · · meas. 15-16

                                                              4 meas.

1 again becomes the leader.
2 and 3 raise joined hands.
2 turns under her L arm.
3 turns under her R arm.
1 walks forward and under.
Continue to hold hands as formerly.

III   Repeat II.
1 leads.
Leap-step-together forward twice · · · · · · · · · · meas. 17-18
Turn under · · · · · · · · · · · · · · meas. 19-20
2 and 3 lead.
Leap-step-together forward twice · · · · · · · · · · meas. 21-22
Turn under again, making 1 the leader · · · · · · · meas. 23-24

                                                              8 meas.

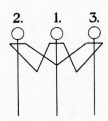

IV   Quickly take crossed position of hands for next figure.

2 and 3 bring hands down in front of 1. This makes crossed position.

1 joins her R hand to 2's R.

1 joins her L hand to 3's L.

2 joins her L hand to 3's R.

All leap-step-together forward	meas. 25
Leap-step-together back	meas. 26
Run forward and hold	meas. 27-28

4 meas.

Leap-step-together back	meas. 29
Leap-step-together forward	meas. 30
Run back and hold	meas. 31-32

4 meas.

Finish in this position:—

2 and 3 raise clasped hands in point above head of 1.

1 continues to hold R hand of 2 and L hand of 3.

Play

WALTZ—SCHUBERT
Op. 9b, No. 15

Photography by Gates

MARCH

March

"Modern" dance composition for 8 girls

Music—March—Alexis
Hollaender, Op. 39, No. 1

Costume—Flame colored rayon tunic. Square neck, fitted with darts at waist-line, skirt slightly flared and coming above knee. See picture.

Fig. I   Girls stand in position of diagram, 3 U L on diagonal, 3 U R on diagonal, 2 U C on straight line. All have arms folded squarely in front of chests.

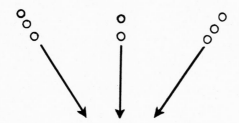

Theme A

2 center girls begin, ct. 1 and take 8 marching or walking steps forward

6 side girls (3 each side) remain in place - - - - (meas. 1-2)

2 center girls take 8 marching steps backward
6 side girls take 8 marching steps forward - - - - (meas. 3-4)   4 meas.

Center girls—8 marching steps forward
Side girls—8 marching steps back - - - - - - (meas. 5-6)

Center girls—8 marching steps back
Side girls—8 marching steps forward - - - - - (meas. 7-8)   4 meas.

All march around according to diagram:—

(1) Side figures march forward diagonally as in 1

(2) March past each other, in semi-circle to U R and L

(3) Walk past each other in 2 straight lines across back stage
At end of (1) 2 center girls walk forward and join line at front, one going to R, one to L
Finish in position for next figure - - - - - - (meas. 9-16)   8 meas.

[181]

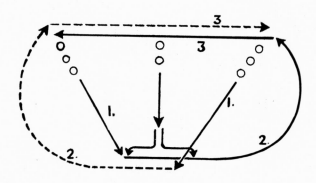

Fig. II 3 each side in triangular formation:—
1 girl in front; 2 girls stand side by side back of 1, inside hands joined
together, outside hands joined to 1, whose arms are swung backward.

(a) Advance separately forward and back on diagonal lines, with:—
Group 1 U L   Theme B
Lunge forward and hold · · · · · · · · (meas. 17)
Walk forward 4 steps · · · · · · · · (meas. 18)
Lunge forward and hold · · · · · · · (meas. 19)
Walk backward 4 and remain in place · · · (meas. 20)   4 meas.

(b) Group 2 U R repeat movement of (a)   (meas. 21-24)   4 meas.

Fig. III Formation—2 straight lines across stage—See picture.
Line I—Arms extended sideward, finger tips pointing upward
Line II—Arms extended straight overhead.

(a) Lines shift alternately R and L:—
Line I—Lunge to R—Draw L up to R 4 times
Line II—Step L—close R to L 4 times · (meas. 25-28)   4 meas.
Repeat—Line I moving to L · · · · · · (meas. 29-32)   4 meas.
Line II moving to R

(b) Position—2 straight lines across stage as in (a)   Theme A
Line I—Hands pointed to hips, elbows triangular.
Line II—Hands placed on top of head, palm down, I hand on
top of other.
Lines shift again:—
Front line walk backward 8
Back line walk forward 8 at same time · · · (meas. 1-2)
Repeat—Front line walk forward 8
Back line walk backward 8 · · · · (meas. 3-4)
Repeat (b) · · · · · · · · · · · (meas. 5-8)   8 meas.

Fig. IV (a) All in one straight line—
Walk forward 4 steps, raising R arm forward, shoulder level.
Walk back 4, raising R arm high above head
Repeat (a) · · · · · · · · · · · (meas. 9-12)   4 meas.

(b) Walk forward 4, raising both arms forward to shoulder level.
Walk back 4, raising both arms above head

Repeat (b) ˏ ˏ ˏ ˏ ˏ ˏ ˏ ˏ ˏ ˏ ˏ (meas. 13-16) 4 meas.

Finish in straight line D S

B Theme

Separate, 3 going to R and 3 to L and walk around according
to diagram:— ˏ ˏ ˏ ˏ ˏ ˏ ˏ ˏ ˏ ˏ ˏ ˏ ˏ (meas. 17-20) 4 meas.

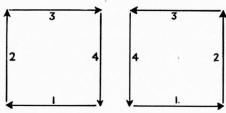

Fig. V   All stand in square formation, finger tips on shoulders, elbows
pointing down front.

Side lines shift, changing places with 4 (step-close) steps

Repeat returning to place ˏ ˏ ˏ ˏ ˏ ˏ ˏ ˏ (meas. 21-24) 4 meas.

Front and back lines shift with 4 walking steps forward and 4
walking steps back ˏ ˏ ˏ ˏ ˏ ˏ ˏ ˏ ˏ ˏ ˏ ˏ (25-28) 4 meas.

All walk backward to straight line ˏ ˏ ˏ ˏ ˏ ˏ ˏ (29-32) 4 meas.

Fig. VI   All in straight line formation U C   Repeat theme B

(a) All face a partner and walk around her, elbows bent to side, hands,
palm up, finger tips pointing outward ˏ ˏ ˏ ˏ ˏ ˏ (17-20) 4 meas.

(b) All six girls walk around in one big circle, arms curving to each side
(21-24) 4 meas.

All walk in 2 small circles—3 girls in each circle

Walk around to original formation at beginning of dance (25-32) 8 meas.

Fig. VII Repeat all of Figure I, ending in same position as at beginning of
dance, except change position of arms

Lift arms upward above head and hold outward in triangular
position.

Repeat theme A

March

ALEXIS HOLLAENDER, Op. 39, № 1

Play AB, AB, BA.

Banners

Oh! Life is a Dance of Banners
   Gaily flying by,
Life is a Dance of Banners
   I pray you hold them high.

Oh! Love your banner madly
   And carry it with joy
And fling the challenge gladly
   To every girl and boy.

Oh! Courage to the dancers
   And strength to keep them all,
For the banners must go on
   Though all the dancers fall.

Each one to his own banner
   To keep it floating high,
For life is dancing onward
   With banners flying by.

Give all you have of beauty
   For when the dance is done,
The banners join together
   To show the cause is won.

L. L.

Part I

A DANCE OF BANNERS
Part IV

Part III

A Dance of Banners

A symbolic dance in four parts

Music, Valses Nobles Op. 77, Nos. 1, 8, 9, 11
Schubert

Costume—Each dancer wears a white silk tunic, draped according to classic lines and coming above the knee, elastic at waist.

Scarf—Each dancer has a brilliant red scarf 1 yard wide and 2 yards long. (3 yards long for college students.)

Leader—Has similar scarf, but is costumed in a red tunic, with silver ribbon crossed over shoulders to waist line and silver ribbon band on forehead.

Part I—For six dancers. Part I is symbolic of dedication to the cause and loyalty to the leader.

Introduction—Leader is standing U L, scarf held in L hand. Scarf is held by two corners and falls in curving line, lengthwise on floor.

Five dancers enter from D R. They are holding scarfs widthwise, above heads, one hand at each corner. They leap in, one at a time, diagonally across stage to U L, scarfs floating in back. As each dancer reaches leader, she kneels (one knee on floor) and flinging scarf high above head, she lets the opposite end from the one she holds, fall in a curving line on floor in front of leader, as a symbol of dedication and loyalty. See picture page 189, part I.

All dancers end in diagonal line, kneeling in front of leader.

Floor Plan

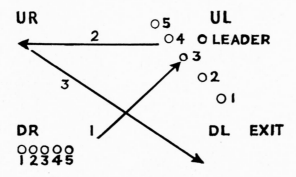

Leader raises R hand in gesture of salute, then holding scarf in L hand, flings it forward, over head and back. (This gesture means that the dancers must lift their banners and go forward.)

Leader separates two corners of scarf and ends with scarf held widthwise in both hands, high above head and floating in back.

Five dancers, still holding scarfs in both hands, rise, turning under R arms. This leaves scarfs floating in back and dancers facing in opposite direction. Nos. 3 and 4 open the way for leader to come through.

Leader leads the line out. All leap out, following leader in line formation. Leap straight across to U R.

Turn and leap diagonally across to D L and exit.

Musical directions.

Schubert Valses Nobles, Op. 77, No. 1

Part I   First dancer leaps in ˏ ˏ ˏ ˏ ˏ ˏ ˏ ˏ ˏ ˏ ˏ ˏ (meas. 1-4)   4 meas.
Kneel, count 1 and 2, meas. 4

Second dancer leaps in ˏ ˏ ˏ ˏ ˏ ˏ ˏ ˏ ˏ ˏ (meas. 5-8)   4 meas.
Start leaping, meas. 4, count 3
Kneel, meas. 8

Third dancer leaps in and kneels   ˏ ˏ ˏ ˏ ˏ ˏ (meas. 1-4)   4 meas.
Repeat music as written
Same as for dancer 1

Fourth dancer leaps in and kneels ˏ ˏ ˏ ˏ ˏ ˏ (meas. 5-8)   4 meas.
Music same as for dancer 2

Fifth dancer leaps in ˏ ˏ ˏ ˏ ˏ ˏ ˏ ˏ ˏ ˏ (meas. 9-12)   4 meas.
Kneel, meas. 12, counts 1 and 2

Leader salutes, meas. 12, count 3 ˏ ˏ ˏ ˏ ˏ ˏ (meas. 12-13)
Meas. 13, counts 1 and 2
Leader lifts scarf, meas. 13, count 3 ˏ ˏ ˏ ˏ ˏ (meas. 13-14)
Meas. 14, counts 1 and 2

Five dancers rise and turn
Leader changes scarf to both hands ˏ ˏ ˏ ˏ ˏ ˏ ˏ ˏ ˏ ˏ ˏ 4 meas.
Meas. 14, count 3
Meas. 15 and 16
All leap out   ˏ ˏ ˏ ˏ ˏ ˏ ˏ ˏ ˏ ˏ ˏ ˏ (meas. 9-16)   8 meas.

Part II   The position of dancers with scarf is based on Cot's painting, "The Storm." Here, it is symbolic of unity and comradeship. Two people are dancing under the same banner and working toward the same ideal.

Two dancers, Couple 1 enter from U R. They are dancing side by side and have their arms around each other's waists. They are holding one scarf lengthwise, high above their heads, with outside arms. (One dancer holds scarf with R hand. Other dancer holds scarf with L hand.) They leap around, following floor pattern of diagram. When they have reached U C (marked 8 on diagram), 4 dancers, two couples join them. Couple

1 enters from U R. Couple 2 enters from U L. All six leap to D C and finish in straight line formation, holding scarfs high above heads.

Floor Pattern

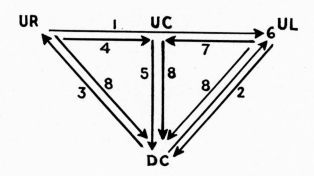

Schubert Valses Nobles, Op. 77, No. 9

Couple 1

1 Leap straight across stage from U R to U L ⌐ ⌐   (meas. 1-8)   8 meas

2 Leap diagonally down stage from U L to D C ⌐   (meas. 9-12)   4 meas.

3 Leap diagonally up stage from D C to U R ⌐ ⌐   (meas. 13-16)   4 meas.

4 Leap straight across from U R to U C ⌐ ⌐ ⌐   (meas. 17-20)   4 meas.

5 Leap straight down from U C to D C ⌐ ⌐ ⌐   (meas. 21-24)   4 meas.

6 Leap diagonally up stage from D C to U L ⌐ ⌐   (meas. 25-28)   4 meas.

7 Leap straight across from U L to U C ⌐ ⌐ ⌐ ⌐   (meas. 29-32)   4 meas.

8 Couple 1 leap from U C to D C
  Couple 2 leap from U R to D C
  Couple 3 leap from U L to D C ⌐ ⌐ ⌐ ⌐ ⌐   (meas. 33-36)   4 meas.

———————

36 meas.

Part III   For two dancers

Music—Valses Nobles Op. 77, No. 8
Dancer I Part A
Dancer II Part B

Oh! Courage to the dancers
And strength to keep them all,
For the banners must go on
Though all the dancers fall.

First dancer enters U L and dances across stage to U R. She dances in circle and falls U C.

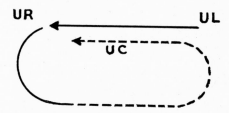

UR ←← UL

UC

She may be thought of as injured, dead, defeated or as having gone away from the leader and fallen in her own lack of strength to sustain her ideal.

She holds scarf by one corner in R hand and gives it a little jerk with accent of music.

1   Leap R—Step L—Step R · · · · · · · · · · · · meas. 1
        Leap L—Step R—Step L · · · · · · · · · · · · meas. 2
        Leap R—Leap L—Leap R · · · · · · · · · · · meas. 3
        Leap L—Step R—Step L · · · · · · · · · · · meas. 4
        Leap R—Step L—Step R · · · · · · · · · · · meas. 5
        Leap L—Step R—Step L · · · · · · · · · · · meas. 6
        Leap R—Leap L—Leap R · · · · · · · · · · · meas. 7
        Jump, feet together and hold · · · · · · · · · · meas. 8

                                             8 meas.

Repeat A music as written.

2   Dancer I, still holding scarf by one corner in R hand, brings scarf
        forward, up over head and back, making backward curve.   meas. 1 count 1
        Extend left hand forward and walk two steps   count 2, 3
        Repeat (a) · · · · · · · · · · · · · · · meas. 2
        Walk three steps · · · · · · · · · · · · · meas. 3
        Fling scarf up and back. Hold, feet together · · · · · meas. 4
        Repeat (a) · · · · · · · · · · · · · · meas. 5
        Repeat (a) · · · · · · · · · · · · · · meas. 6
        Standing, feet together on tip-toe, curve scarf back, up and forward   meas. 7
        Lunge back and fall · · · · · · · · · · · · meas. 8

                                             8 meas.

3 (a)   Second dancer enters U L and walks straight across to U C, where
        she sees her fallen comrade and pauses. See picture page 189, part III.
        Dancer walks. Step-hold · · · · · · · · count 1   meas. 9
        Step · · · · · · · · · · · · · · · count 2
        Step · · · · · · · · · · · · · · · count 3
        Repeat step-hold step-step · · · · · · · · · meas. 10
        Three even steps · · · · · · · · · · · · meas. 11
        Step-hold. See fallen comrade · · · · · · · · meas. 12

Stand, D S (Left) knee bent, forming triangle, arms outstretched
to each side, palms down.

(b) Lunge D S (Left) foot. Torso twist, shoulders facing front and
   feet pointing to side · · · · · · · · · · · · · · meas. 13
   Arms form two triangles. Bring hands over eyes, palms touching.
   Kneel on U S (R) knee, hands still over eyes · · · · · · · meas. 14
   Bring L knee down. Take position, kneeling on both knees. Knees
   together on floor. Back straight. Uncover eyes by bringing hands
   out to each side · · · · · · · · · · · · · · meas. 15
   Same position, kneeling. Reach up with both arms, as though
   asking for strength. Keep knees pointing to side, shoulders facing
   forward, torso twist · · · · · · · · · · · · meas. 16
   Sit back on heels. Reach up again with both arms, hands outstretched, palms up · · · · · · · · · · · · · · meas. 17
   Turn palms down. Bring hands down, arms outstretched, gesture
   of hovering over comrade in attitude of tenderness · · · · · meas. 18
   Still sitting back on heels, knees together on floor, pick up scarf
   in both hands and hold it high above head like a garland, scarf
   evenly divided in thirds · · · · · · · · · · · · meas. 19
   Rise · · · · · · · · · · · · · · · · · · · meas. 20

(c) Walk out, holding scarf like a garland, high above head. Torso
   twist. Keep shoulders forward, feet pointing to side, body in two-
   dimensional design.
   Step-hold · · · · · · · · · · · · · · · · count 1 meas. 21
   Step · · · · · · · · · · · · · · · · · · count 2
   Step · · · · · · · · · · · · · · · · · · count 3
   Repeat Step-hold. Step-step · · · · · · · · · · · meas. 22
   Three even steps · · · · · · · · · · · · · · · meas. 23
   Exit U R · · · · · · · · · · · · · · · · · · meas. 24

   ───────────
   16 meas.

Part IV   Three Couples

Music—Schubert Valses Nobles Op. 77, No. 11

Symbolic of a victorious ideal won by the spirit of unity, harmony and cooperation on the part of the group.

> Give all you have of beauty
> For when the dance is done,
> The banners join together
> To show the cause is won.

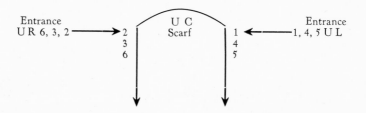

Couple I

1   Dancer No. 1 enters U L with a scarf, held widthwise in both
hands, high above head and floating in back.   At same time, dancer
2 enters (without scarf) U R

Both run U C where they meet   ⸲ ⸲ ⸲ ⸲ ⸲ ⸲ ⸲ ⸲ ⸲ ⸲ ⸲ ⸲   meas. 1

Dancer with scarf, flings it up and forward to partner, standing
opposite   ⸲   meas. 2

Partner catches other end and both (each holding 2 ends) draw
ends together and puff scarf up, making an arch   ⸲ ⸲ ⸲ ⸲ ⸲ ⸲   meas. 3

Both run forward. See picture page 153, part IV   ⸲ ⸲ ⸲ ⸲ ⸲ ⸲   meas. 4

_____

4 meas.

Couple II

2   Dancer No. 3 runs in U R with scarf and pauses U C where she
meets No. 4 who runs in at same time from U L   ⸲ ⸲ ⸲ ⸲ ⸲ ⸲   meas. 5

Dancer 3 flings opposite end of scarf to dancer 4   ⸲ ⸲ ⸲ ⸲ ⸲ ⸲   meas. 6

Both make arch with scarf   ⸲ ⸲ ⸲ ⸲ ⸲ ⸲ ⸲ ⸲ ⸲ ⸲ ⸲ ⸲ ⸲   meas. 7

Still, holding scarf high above heads, both run forward under arch,
made by 1 and 2 and pause on parallel lines with them   ⸲ ⸲ ⸲ ⸲   meas. 8

_____

4 meas

While dancers 3 and 4 are entering and forming figure, dancers
1 and 2:—
Lower scarf ⁻ ⁻ ⁻ ⁻ ⁻ ⁻ ⁻ ⁻ ⁻ ⁻ ⁻ ⁻ ⁻ ⁻ ⁻ ⁻ meas. 5-6
Lift scarf in arch and hold ⁻ ⁻ ⁻ ⁻ ⁻ ⁻ ⁻ ⁻ ⁻ ⁻ ⁻ ⁻ meas. 7-8

_____

4 meas.

Couple III

3 Dancer No. 5 with scarf enters from U L. Dancer No. 6 enters
from U R. Both meet U C ⁻ ⁻ ⁻ ⁻ ⁻ ⁻ ⁻ ⁻ ⁻ ⁻ ⁻ ⁻ meas. 9
No. 5 flings opposite end of her scarf to No. 6 ⁻ ⁻ ⁻ ⁻ ⁻ ⁻ meas. 10
Both puff scarf up in arch ⁻ ⁻ ⁻ ⁻ ⁻ ⁻ ⁻ ⁻ ⁻ ⁻ ⁻ ⁻ meas. 11
Both run under the two arches formed by Dancers (1 and 2) and
dancers (3 and 4) and pause on parallel lines with them ⁻ ⁻ ⁻ meas. 12

_____

4 meas.

While couple 5 and 6 are entering, couple 1 and 2, couple 3 and 4
do following movements:—
Lower scarf ⁻ ⁻ ⁻ ⁻ ⁻ ⁻ ⁻ ⁻ ⁻ ⁻ ⁻ ⁻ ⁻ ⁻ ⁻ ⁻ meas. 9-10
Lift scarf in arch ⁻ ⁻ ⁻ ⁻ ⁻ ⁻ ⁻ ⁻ ⁻ ⁻ ⁻ ⁻ ⁻ ⁻ meas. 11-12

_____

4 meas.

4 All six dancers are now in place on stage, 3 on one side, 3 on
opposite side. Face partner.
All lower scarf ⁻ ⁻ ⁻ ⁻ ⁻ ⁻ ⁻ ⁻ ⁻ ⁻ ⁻ ⁻ ⁻ ⁻ ⁻ meas. 13
All lift scarf in arch ⁻ ⁻ ⁻ ⁻ ⁻ ⁻ ⁻ ⁻ ⁻ ⁻ ⁻ ⁻ ⁻ meas. 14
Hold scarf in arch ⁻ ⁻ ⁻ ⁻ ⁻ ⁻ ⁻ ⁻ ⁻ ⁻ ⁻ ⁻ ⁻ ⁻ meas. 15-16

_____

4 meas.

Leader enters U C and runs under arch D C ⁻ ⁻ ⁻ ⁻ ⁻ ⁻ ⁻ meas. 15
Leader holds, arms lifted in gesture of victory ⁻ ⁻ ⁻ ⁻ ⁻ ⁻ meas. 16

A Dance of Banners

Part I

Valses Nobles
FR. SCHUBERT
Op. 77, № 1

A DANCE OF BANNERS
Part II

Valses Nobles
FR. SCHUBERT
Op.77, № 9

A DANCE OF BANNERS
A Part III

Valse Nobles
FR. SCHUBERT
Op.77, № 8

The Day

"The day will bring some lovely thing",
  I say it over each new dawn,
"Some gay, adventurous thing
  To hold against my heart when it is gone."
And so I rise and go to meet
  The day with wings upon my feet.

No day has ever failed me quite.
  Before the greyest day is done,
I come upon some misty bloom
  Or late line of crimson sun.
Each night I pause, remembering
  Some gay, adventurous, lovely thing.

GRACE NOLL CROWELL

THE DAY

The Day

Dance for any number, preferably 5 or 7, inspired by the poem "The Day" by Grace Noll Crowell. Further reference "Isadora Duncan—Twenty-four Studies" by Arnold Genthe.

Music—Schubert Waltzes.
Part 1—Deutsche Tanze, Op. 33, No. 7.
Part 2—Walzer Op. 9 a No. 14.
Part 3—Walzer Op. 9 b No. 18.

Lines 1-2

Part I When curtain opens, girls are lying in a diagonal line, as if asleep.
Take position of first figure in picture. Waltz I
Raise head as in second figure.
Take first position again · - · - · - · - · - · - · (1-4) 4 meas.
Come up to reclining position again, L leg extended.
R knee drawn up on floor, L hand on L knee—R hand on floor.
Take position of figure 4 · - · - · - · - · - · - (5-8) 4 meas.
Take position of figure 5 (except extend L leg).
Change from closed to open position by moving hands only.
Place L hand on R knee and R hand on floor in back.
Take position of figure 7 · - · - · - · - · - · - (9-12) 4 meas.
Turn to R side, place R knee on floor.
Come up on both knees and turn to R.
Raise L knee and extend R hand, as if giving something to someone.
Rise to full height and walk to R. Stand on tip-toe R arm raised high above head, as if reaching upward toward something.
(13-16) 4 meas.

Lines 5-6

Part II All face R. Waltz II
Hop L, lifting R knee high, curving hands in to breasts, palms in.
Step down on R, lift L off floor (at same time) in back and lift both arms above head, elbows curved.
Swing L forward and run in circle to R, 7 steps, starting L (1-4) 4 meas.
Repeat 3 times · - · - · - · - · - · - · (5-16) 12 meas.
Finish in semi-circle U C.
Lines 7-9
All face to R.
Hop R—Lunge L—Make gesture of picking flower with L hand.

[205]

Whirl to L on tip-toes as if smelling flower   - - - -   (17-20)   4 meas.
Repeat movement to L - - - - - - - - - -   (21-24)   4 meas.
All whirl to R, arms curved above head.   Repeat music
Make gesture of scattering petals - - - - - - - -   (17-20)   4 meas.
Repeat, whirling to L - - - - - - - - - -   (21-24)   4 meas.

Line 10

Part III   All face forward U C.   Waltz III

Walk slowly forward as if looking at sun-set.
Begin with arms at side. Lift arms gradually forward. Curve arms
above head, hands extended outward. Open arms to shoulder level.
Turn palms down and lower arms - - - - - - - -   (1-8)   8 meas.
Lines 11-12
Still facing audience, kneel on both knees.
Sit on floor, facing R (Opposite from part I) - - - - - - -   4 meas.
Take position of figure 6—Lines 3-4
Take position of figure III.
Finish with position of figure I - - - - - - - -   (9-16)   4 meas.

—————————

8 meas.

The Day

FR. SCHUBERT
Op. 33, № 7

Torches

Torches, burning torches,
   Flung across the sky,
Torches, flaming torches,
   Who will hold them high?

Eager hands will catch them,
   Shining eyes will see;
Aspiring souls will sing
   Songs of ecstasy.

Lights of radiant spirits
   Fill us with desire
To kindle pallid torches
   With a heavenly fire.

Torches, burning torches,
   Flung across the sky,
Torches, flaming torches,
   Who will hold them high?

L. L.

The Torch of Beauty